ED BRUBAKER: CONVERSATIONS

Conversations with Comic Artists   M. Thomas Inge, General Editor

Ed Brubaker: Conversations

Edited by Terrence Wandtke

University Press of Mississippi   Jackson

www.upress.state.ms.us

The University Press of Mississippi is a member of the Association of
    American University Presses.

First printing 2016
∞
Library of Congress Cataloging-in-Publication Data

Brubaker, Ed, author.
 [Interviews. Selections]
 Ed Brubaker : conversations / Edited by Terrence Wandtke.
    pages cm. — (Conversations with comic artists)
Collection of interviews originally published in various sources.
Includes index.
ISBN 978-1-4968-0550-8 (cloth : alk. paper) — ISBN 978-1-4968-0551-5
    (ebook) 1. Brubaker, Ed—Interviews. 2. Cartoonists—United States—
    Interviews. I. Wandtke, Terrence R., editor. II. Title.
PN6727.B77Z46 2016
741.5'973—dc23

                                        2015032547

British Library Cataloging-in-Publication Data available

Books by Ed Brubaker

Top Shelf:

(The Complete) Lowlife (Slave Labor, Caliber, Aeon)

Alternative:

At the Seams

Detour

Fantagraphics:

An Accidental Death (Dark Horse)

Vertigo:

Deadenders

Sandman Presents: Deadboy Detectives

Vertigo Visions: Prez, Smells Like Teen President

DC:

Batman: Bruce Wayne, Murderer

Batman: Gotham Noir

Batman: The Man Who Laughs

Catwoman

Gotham Central

Wildstorm:

The Authority: Revolution

Point Blank

Sleeper

Marvel:

Books of Doom

Captain America

Captain America and Bucky

Daredevil

The Immortal Iron Fist

The Marvels Project

Secret Avengers

Steve Rogers: Super Soldier

X-Men: Deadly Genesis

Winter Soldier

Icon:

Criminal: Vols. 1 & 2

Criminal: The Last of the Innocent

Criminal: The Sinners

Incognito

Image:

The Fade Out

Fatale

Scene of the Crime (Vertigo)

Velvet

This list is in a rough chronological order but in some cases, publishers are the most current (rather than the original listed in parentheses). Subtitles are maintained if the original series contained a subtitle or Brubaker's runs on a series are now more familiar with the subtitle.

CONTENTS

INTRODUCTION

> "I was never one of those people who automatically dismissed genre
> stuff. I dismissed mysteries because it seemed stupid to read stuff with
> a solution at the end, like a crossword puzzle, until I actually read some
> good ones, like Hammett and Chandler. You realize that people can
> actually do anything within those boundaries."
> —Ed Brubaker (Groth and Spurgeon 73)

As a prolific and talented comic book creator, Ed Brubaker occupies an interesting position in the contemporary comics scene as a self-described
pulp writer, devoted to the conventions of superhero and crime stories. He
describes himself as such in a time when contemporary comics are now often distanced from their pulp origins by creators who prefer to connect the
medium to more culturally approved art and design traditions. In contrast,
Brubaker's work on company-owned properties like Batman and Captain
America and creator-owned series like *Criminal* and *Fatale* lives up to the traditional expectations for superhero and crime stories, respectively. And yet,
as Brubaker acknowledges, he likes to extend genre boundaries and experiment with how far he can extend those boundaries before the genres need to
be called something else. Moreover, Brubaker layers his stories with a keen
self-awareness, using his expansive knowledge of American comic book history to invigorate his work and challenge the dividing line between low and
high art. In this way, Brubaker works not only as a popular entertainer but
also as a self-conscious artist and a critical theorist. And while he tends not to
refer to himself as a theorist or situate himself within any specific theoretical
framework, Brubaker's work is often described as postmodern by people who
may or may not understand the term.

In any case, Brubaker is an artist of intersections and feels comfortable
with his position as such. Aside from modernism and postmodernism, some
of those intersections to which he blatantly makes reference include the
aforementioned pulp and art as well as biography and fiction, independence

and incorporation, superhero and crime stories, print and digital formats (for comics), and approval and controversy (from fans, critics, and the general public). With effortless and concurrent references to Milan Kundera's *The Art of the Novel*, Sal Buscema's *Captain America*, and (his uncle) John Paxton's *Crossfire*, he artfully negotiates between the intersections that form the basis for his life as a creator. While some may argue about the originality and genius of the artist, a strict notion of the "new" has generally been jettisoned in the modern age of comics. In its place is the artist who makes great things because that artist can more fully recognize, choose, revise, and reinterpret influences. Ed Brubaker has that ability to negotiate the complexity of the currents that now feed the contemporary comic scene, currents that include not only comics but other media forms as well. For Brubaker, those currents clearly include comics material such as kid-friendly *Archie* comics and controversial EC crime comics, classic Marvel superhero comics and revisionist superhero comics such as *The Dark Knight* and *Watchmen*; comics criticism ranging from that of the infamous *Seduction of the Innocent* to the groundbreaking *The Comics Journal*; film sources including the cult classic *Harry in Your Pocket* and the self-conscious *Kiss Kiss Bang Bang*; and fiction inspirations in the seminal crime fiction of Dashiel Hammett and the deconstructive crime fiction of Paul Auster. All of this results in sophisticated work in comics (and more recently, in film) that simultaneously lives up to and works beyond expectations. Brubaker is part of a generation encouraging the common reader of comics to expect a more sophisticated narrative and visual experience; working consistently with illustrators that know him well, Brubaker's work has the potential to retrain the reader to think about comics more broadly in terms of cultural context.

For instance, in *Lowlife* (1991–1996), Brubaker begins his career with a variation on the autobiographical art comics like *American Splendor* and *Palookaville*. Painfully confessional like the work of Harvey Pekar and following the life of a slacker like the emerging fiction subgenre focusing on Generation X, Brubaker refines his artistry and experiments with visual representation to create symbols and narrative unity that extends beyond strict realism. In *Sleeper* (2003–2005), Brubaker explores the Wildstorm universe, created to nurture independent creativity but for the most part replicating the tropes of mainstream superhero comics. However, when the sleeper of the title, Holden Carver, lives in this grim and gritty superhero world as a double agent, his cover story exposes the arbitrary nature of the superhero standards of good and evil with excessive, metafictive flair. In *Daredevil* (2006–2009), he furthers the work of Frank Miller and Brian Michael Bendis on the series, informed by hard-boiled detective fiction and film noir. In the process, he makes Daredevil into one of the most tragically depressed characters in contemporary superhero comics: no longer a Raymond Chandler knight in disguise but a Jim Thompson killer whose adherence to conventional virtue is lost in his anger and frustration. And in *Criminal* (2006–2011), he offers desperate crime stories told by the desperate (and sometimes deranged) criminals. Installments like "Bad Night" and "The Last of the Innocent" implement contrasting comic art styles to represent parts of the fractured consciousness of the protagonists and, quite ambitiously, analyze American comic book history including the supposedly benign influence of Dick Tracy. And with a clear sense of the lost world before the Comics Code, "The Last of the Innocent" rejects the myth of the innocence and juvenility of 1950s culture supposedly represented by the early history of comics like *Archie*.

With a multilayered approach to his work, Brubaker remains a pulp writer in the sense that he entertains with highly subversive and intelligent work in a medium still somewhat outside the restrictions placed on media clearly identified as high art. With an awareness of how to satisfy a wide audience, Brubaker manages to revise his genres of choice in ways that transform traditional expectations for superhero and crime stories in ways as significant as Robert Mayer's *Superfolks* and Haruki Murakami's *The Wind-Up Bird Chronicle*. Brubaker demonstrates his self-conscious methodology in his interviews that deserve to be showcased as worthwhile conversations in their own right and as objects of study for readers, scholars, and researchers.

FROM MILD-MANNERED SLACKER TO FULL-FLEDGED CRIMINAL

Ed Brubaker began his career in increments, first as an amateur, then independent, then mainstream comics creator, and he did this at a rather interesting time in comic book history—especially if one is considering the ways that multiple influences on comics seem to be most apparent within the industry. Like many comic book readers of his time, Brubaker became a comic book reader in the 1970s thanks to a box of comics owned by his father that included both Marvel superhero and EC crime comics (Groth and Spurgeon 61). However, his tastes would alter and grow into their maturity as the American comic book industry changed in notable ways in the 1980s and 1990s. After decades of content shaped by the Comics Code and a few major companies, the growth of the direct market and the black and white explosion of the

1980s encouraged comic book creators more than ever before to think beyond the confines of superhero stories written for adolescents. Starting a job in a direct market comic book store in the mid-1980s, Brubaker would be well aware of these changes and the creative thought that they encouraged; already an amateur comic book writer, he read independent black and white comics that defied easy genre classification such as *Cerebus* and *Love and Rockets*. And Brubaker was not only aware of the emerging critical culture associated with the direct market via *The Comics Journal* but he also participated in this mode of thought as a critic as well as a creator. Reflecting on this time period, Brubaker states, "When I was in my twenties, I wrote reviews and articles for a living, while writing and drawing my own comics on the side, because it was just something I had to do" (Hood). As described by comics scholar Bradford W. Wright, it was a time that favored the comic book writer as an artist: "New independent publishers started to target the direct market, and most of these offered creative autonomy" (Wright 262). With discussions of comics as art and creators as rights-holders informing his ideas, Brubaker made overtures into the new independent scene with relatively unsuccessful titles such as *Pajama Chronicles* (1987) and *Purgatory USA* (1989), both published by the new, small publisher Slave Labor. Relatively lacking in terms of their mastery of basic narrative and design principles, they nevertheless demonstrate Brubaker's interest in story content outside the framework of established traditional superhero tropes.

His significant critical breakthrough would come in 1991 with *Lowlife*, initially published by Slave Labor and then Caliber. It would neatly fit a definition of "alternative comics" developed by comics scholars Randy Duncan and Matthew Smith, who describe them as "usually created by a single cartoonist and present[ing] a very personal vision . . . [with] emphasis on the author more than on characters. . . . due to the radical change in distribution . . . [alternatives were] sold side-by-side with mainstream comics" (Duncan and Smith 66–67). Influenced by a wave of autobiographical comics favored by supporters of the "new comics" like *The Comics Journal*, Brubaker demonstrates his flair for dialogue and his interest in the dark corners of everyday life. Although not strictly autobiographical, Brubaker drew on elements of his own life and crafted a monologue-heavy approach that recalled the approach of Harvey Pecker's *American Splendor*. Due to his future identification as a crime writer, the most consistent reference by comics readers is to the first story in the series, "A Life of Crime," a series of related vignettes that look at Thomas Booker's minor criminal acts leading to an armed robbery. Far from being a *Crime Does Not Pay* making-of-the-criminal story, "A Life of Crime"

Fig. 1: A massive fire allows Tommy and Sunny to reconnect in a tepid way in the midst of their long breakup in *Lowlife* #5. (From *Lowlife* #5 by Ed Brubaker © Ed Brubaker; originally published by Aeon in 1995; available in *The Complete Lowlife*)

stresses Tommy's own ill feelings during a bad acid trip toward the successful crime and amplifies it with a comparison to crimes committed by others. Balancing the thoughts of the character with his first person narrative, we are exposed to Tommy's desperation: "I held a gun on someone . . . My God . . . I have no soul . . . I was overcome with a feeling of emptiness . . . What was the use of it all? The whole world was just a random series of cruelties" (Brubaker, *A Complete* 9–10). However, the motivating factor in the story is less the psychology of criminal behavior than the relationships that it endangered and frailty of human connection (something that ultimately became the enduring theme of *Lowlife*).

Due to the speculator market that was formed in the late 1980s and early 1990s, Slave Labor often had remarkable sales for a small publisher, but the market that enabled them as publishers of low print run series would come to an end around 1993 when the speculator bubble burst. Without much financial benefit from *Lowlife*, Brubaker committed to continued work on the series, eventually consisting of five issues, with other publishers over the course of five years. In addition to his commitment to his own creation, he would refine his cartooning style over the course of the series. While he may have recognized the limitations of his own skills as an illustrator (concurrently and subsequently almost always working as a writer), Brubaker shows a greater sense of complexity with his visual presentation; his art becomes shaped by a thicker brushwork style, perspectives of characters are presented in subjective fantasies, and creative angles are used to emphasize the importance of images as counterpoint to monologue. For instance, in "The Girlfriend," Tommy's desire for his cheating girlfriend is literally portrayed through a violent sexual encounter but also symbolically portrayed in a more poignant way after she leaves him; with a meager sense of optimism expressed in the second-to-last panel, Tommy decides to clean up his apartment and in last panel, Brubaker offers a wordless presentation of the overgrown and dying garden started outside by his girlfriend. Brubaker acknowledges the continuing autobiographical influence on his work throughout his career but from the start with *Lowlife*, he argues for the conscious artistic choices that are necessarily part of his retelling of his own story: "I've always found it funny that reviewers act as if autobiographical work doesn't go through any sort of creative process at all, and that the guy who shows himself being cheap all the time, and hitting his girlfriend, thinks he's showing himself at his finest and it's just an accident that it got put down on paper" (Brubaker, *A Complete* i).

At the same time that he worked on *Lowlife*, Brubaker would collaborate with other artists on short stories for *Dark Horse Presents* such as "Burning Man" in 1991 and the three-issue arc of "An Accidental Death" in 1992. Like other smaller publishers at that time, Dark Horse allowed creators to own their creations but, unlike many smaller publishers at that time, had a business plan and policies that made it likely to weather the storm from the death of the speculator market (Duncan and Smith 73–74). Quite notably, Dark Horse published several works by Frank Miller, including *Sin City*, debuting in *Dark Horse Presents* in 1991, putting Brubaker in the company of a comic book celebrity. Moreover, Dark Horse encouraged not only Miller but also Brubaker and other writers of the time to bring back crime comics traditions in the anthology format associated with the genre in the 1950s. "An

Accidental Death" was a major accomplishment, garnering attention for his work from critics and fans alike. Working with Eric Shanower whose illustration realistically represented the tale of urban disillusionment, Brubaker began to develop and refine his longstanding preference for the crime genre—at that time influenced by EC Comics and Jim Thompson novels (but more subtle and humane). In an explicit way, the story continued to use Brubaker's own life as source material with the main character as a teenager living at the Guantanamo Bay Naval Base (as a boy, Brubaker lived there at Gitmo with his father, a naval intelligence officer). However, as a story of a murder and its cover-up, it also departs more significantly than *Lowlife*. Although Brubaker would later be frustrated by the amount of words used (especially in first person narration) in his early work (Brubaker, *Scene* 112), "An Accidental Death" demonstrates an awareness of the importance of images. With wordless panels regularly serving as the frame for the three parts of the story, Brubaker forms a counterpoint to the heavy narration of the story that, for instance, emphasizes the reaction of the main character in fear of recognition in wordless panels.

In terms of the story itself, the narrator, Charlie, and his friend, Frank, are peeping through windows of homes on the base and see a female classmate changing, someone who Frank says he then is dating. Thereafter, Charlie suspects Frank is inventing an elaborate fantasy about his new romantic relationship with her, and one night Frank leads him to the girl's dead body (another effective use of a wordless panel, large and with an aerial, almost cinematic, perspective). Telling a story of how she fell out of a tree where they were sitting, Frank convinces Charlie to help him hide the body. Eventually, Charlie confesses and Frank is caught and nonfatally shot. In the end, Brubaker returns to the flash-forward frame and, in Charlie's narration, demonstrates Charlie's self-protective tendencies and the limitations of an awareness informed by nostalgia: "I guess I hurt a lot of people by going along with Frank but you just don't expect your best friend to be a psycho . . . sure it happens all over the place now . . . but this was a long time ago and things like that just didn't happen" (Brubaker, "An Accidental Death, Part Three" 31). Again, with a focus on relationships and the anxiety associated with crime, Brubaker develops a story that sets forth the ease of committing crime, the uncertainty of criminal motive and responsibility, and the gulf between one individual's perspective and the truth of another's life. Thanks to this story and others of the same ilk, Brubaker was associated with writers like Brian Azzarello, Brian Michael Bendis, and Greg Rucka, who were hailed as the new crime writers of the new comics scene (Bendis i). As the term comic noir was thrown around, Brubaker would react to the mention of this film tradition in this way: "I don't know how much any specific film influenced my work, though, it's more just the themes and the tone of noir that seeps into some of my stuff" (O'Shea). While it may or may not feature hard-boiled detectives and femmes fatale, Brubaker's work seemed to allude to the existential dread at the root of the subgenre.

With "An Accidental Death" nominated for an Eisner in 1993, Brubaker began to receive other, more sizable offers and soon did work for Vertigo. His earliest work for the adult imprint of DC Comics is an interesting, trippy misfire showcasing the son of Prez Rickard, a teenage president character created by Joe Simon: *Prez: Smells Like Teen President* (1995); synthesizing some of his early experimentation with the absurd premise of the obscure character, Brubaker developed a work that made a political statement but didn't strike a chord with readers. However, his time with Vertigo would eventually lead to his first great extended crime story, *Scene of the Crime* (1999), demonstrating not only his mastery of crime tropes but also his self-conscious treatment of those tropes. Although the concept of the graphic novel (an extended, non-serialized narrative comic book) had been around for quite some time, the reality of the graphic novel took shape in the 1980s with higher quality printing, collections, and large single-volume works published by mainstream and independent publishers (Duncan and Smith 70–71). Although originally published in four issues, the arc of the story clearly extended over the course of the series with a pace that showed Brubaker's facility as a storyteller beyond the single-issue, episodic storytelling that was his history up to that point. Entering more explicitly into the genre of crime fiction with the private eye story of *Scene of the Crime*, Brubaker was dealing with crime fiction expectations shaped by fiction, film, and comics. The expectations shaped by comics may have been the most indistinct since the genre had disappeared in the 1950s thanks to the Fredric Wertham's campaign, the Kefauver hearings, and the industry's Comics Code. With that history in mind, the reemergence of crime comics would be the most important revolution within the industry to which Brubaker would significantly contribute. In *Crime Comics: The Illustrated History*, Mike Benton describes the consequences of the direct market: "[M]any new publishers who entered the industry in the 1980s and 1990s produced comic books outside of the Comics Code purview. . . . As a result, the 1980s and 1990s saw new opportunities for the crime and detective comic book genre" (Benton 92–93). Of course, Vertigo was a DC imprint but their publication strategies showed the important changes being made to the mainstream in reaction to this new time.

Brubaker took this opportunity not only to evoke the gumshoe traditions of Raymond Chandler and classic film noir but also to harken to the narrative twists and moral ambiguity of EC's *Crime Suspenstories*. However, as in the case of neo-noir *Chinatown*, the gumshoe traditions are repositioned within a contemporary setting; in *Scene of the Crime* Jack Herriman is hired to track down a woman named Maggie (the client's sister), who had been missing for a month and seemingly connected to a suspicious commune. When he finds her, he makes contact, and while he waits to inform his client, the woman is murdered (creating the personal investment more important than justice in noir stories). In addition to resituating the gumshoe detective in less typical time period, he has the protagonist working from the studio of his uncle, Knut; with the uncle using his reputation and work as a crime scene photographer to make a living, Brubaker explores the way crime and elements of the crime story are elevated as art and festishized: "Knut is of course THE Knut Herriman, the famous news and crime scene photographer. He got his start in the forties and fifties when he was just a teenager learning to be in the wrong place at the wrong time—capturing the elements of life most people would like to forget. He rose to fame in the 'art world' in the late fifties when, at a reception, he decked Weegee . . . if the 'art world' loves anything, it's controversy" (Brubaker, *Scene* 8). After a series of double crosses exposing the corruption of the victim's sister among others, the story moves toward a conclusion that fails to offer the closure of typical mysteries and simultaneously emphasizes a sense of distance and of loss. As Jack stares at the crime scene picture of Maggie hanging in his uncle's gallery, he narrates: "Maggie had wanted something simple, just a little piece of the goodnight she had never gotten as a child. What she found was a complicated mess of emotions and anger—a whole family torn apart by its past. It wasn't a unique tragedy by any means, but it was still a tragedy" (Brubaker, *Scene* 90). As becomes typical in Brubaker stories, the only thing left to sustain characters is a series of problematic relationships between troubled and violent people. This series would help Brubaker to more fully realize his realistic but moody visual aesthetic, featuring panels filled with the long shadows and the mise en scene characteristic of film noir supplied by two illustrators who would thereafter become his most regular collaborators: Michael Lark and Sean Phillips.

ON THE RUN FROM THE ALL AMERICAN HERO

With his obvious talents as a writer of crime stories even more evident, DC offered Brubaker the opportunity to work with their most iconic hard-boiled detective: Batman (with a run beginning with *Batman* in 2000, including back-up stories in *Detective Comics* in 2001, co-writing with Geoff Johns in *Batman* in 2002, and writing main stories in *Detective Comics* in 2003). Coordinating with many other writers on other Bat-titles, he most notably distinguished his run with the "Bruce Wayne: Murderer" arc, interesting because it shows Batman potentially outwitted and Bruce Wayne out of costume more than usual. He would work against the popular interpretation of Batman at the time that viewed Batman as the real character and Bruce Wayne as the false identity, the invented alter ego; for Brubaker, this would make Batman terribly underdeveloped and uninteresting (O'Shea). Of course, this notion sets up a particular approach to superheroics that makes the character development of actual people more important than the plot-driven action of superheroes in costume. In addition to rejecting the large panel, "widescreen" approach to superheroes, he would eventually bridle under the restraints of the cross-continuity stories that are unavoidable with a DC character like Batman. With that stated, the distant corners of DC's array of Bat-titles would showcase some of Brubaker's best work to date, including the revamped *Catwoman* and the new *Gotham Central*. Beginning in 2001 with *Catwoman*, Brubaker explores the world of every fanboy's favorite cat burglar, beginning with a notable change: smaller breasts. Although it was often his punch-line answer to the changes he had in mind for Catwoman, it is appropriately descriptive of his departure from the cheesecake, bad girl, teenage fantasy she had become (Contino). Crediting Frank Miller for his sense of her origin via *Batman: Year One*, Brubaker examines the motivation and conflicted psychology of the morally ambiguous protagonist: "The interesting thing to me is, looking at Selina Kyle, she's someone who was orphaned as a kid, raised in the system in some of the worst conditions, ended up on the streets. But she's got to have some capacity for caring. I think she's only shown that, so far, with Batman really. Or in *Batman: Year One*, she showed some compassion for Holly but that was it. So, why doesn't she care about people like her? People who the system doesn't care about, the cops don't care about, and who, really, Batman doesn't care about? That's kind of where I found a place to get Selina's stories from." (Giles).

Through the classic cartoon style of Darwyn Cooke as illustrator, the series evokes and then revises the predecessors of contemporary crime comics like *Dick Tracy* (or more particularly, Siegel and Shuster's *Slam Bradley* who becomes a series regular). With the help of these stylings and characters, Brubaker creates a space within DC continuity but strangely out of time and place with an often compassionate focus on the lives of small-time criminals. Reinventing Catwoman as less of a master thief and more of a crime character, Brubaker also revises the crime story stereotypes of women (who traditionally must be either the good girl or the femme fatale)—with not only Selina Kyle but also a supporting cast of interesting and strong female characters. Of particular note in the early part of his run with *Catwoman* is Holly Robinson, a gay ex-junkie who aids Catwoman by gathering street-level information (perhaps to her own detriment). In "Disguises, Part 1," Brubaker makes a move similar to that of Will Eisner in *The Spirit* and displaces his main character to focus, in this case, more on Holly. With Holly as the narrator, emphasis is placed on the routine danger of discovery and her perspective as a former drug user working in a world that is suffused with illegal narcotics: "And I just can't stop seeing these streets in junkie-vision. 'We're so high.' 'Casual user.' 'I'm a dealer.' 'I'm a junkie.' Or noticing how easy it would be to give in . . . So while I'm really glad you helped me get off these streets, you also put me right back out on them" (Brubaker, *Catwoman* 231). In addition to this departure from the conventional superhero story, Brubaker enhances the complexity of presentation with the use of a personality quiz (usually associated with women's magazines) taken by Holly, used for comic and then dramatic effect in the narrative of the story as a whole.

Also significant in this period would be another street-level crime drama set in Batman's world, *Gotham Central*, his collaboration with fellow writer Greg Rucka: a procedural in the vein of Ed McBain that follows the detectives in the Gotham City police department. The series works as a vehicle to explore the idea that the average worker in the system is ill equipped to contend with the oppressive nature of the "civilized" urban world (a standard crime story trope accentuated by the threat of supervillains). In reference to his conversations with Rucka, Brubaker states: "[W]e realized how cool it would be if we did a comic like this every month. Where it was always about a crime scene where the Joker walked through and killed a bunch of babies. Just seeing the horror from a perspective that . . . You don't see it from Batman's point of view. These people, they do this every day to the point that it becomes a grind. And how angry they must get, and feel powerless that they can't catch these people, but Batman's going to do it" (Sava). In addition, the series portrays with the power of individual perspective to subvert standard assumptions and moral absolutism; while Batman usually is depicted as the valiant outsider, Gotham City detectives see him as the ultimate embodiment of a demoralizing system: regularly finishing a case with his unlimited resources that the detectives had almost closed against all odds. According to Brubaker, he would split writing chores with Greg Rucka loosely on a case-by-case basis, but the constant was realistic horror of supervillains (with the Joker as a sniper and bomber) and detective's diffidence and bursts of anger toward Batman. Michael Lark reteams with Brubaker and emphasizes these elements with great skill in a conversation between Commissioner Michael Akins and Captain Maggie Sawyer taking place after Batman fails to protect an officer from a bombing. Beginning with a depiction of the rooftop conversation, Akins states, "You never doubted Superman was on your side? In Metropolis, I mean? . . . We've got cops dying while we wait for him to save the day. That's just not right." The scene changes to the comatose police officer as Sawyer states, "No, sir, it's not . . ." and then to a bound Joker laughing in his hospital bed as Sawyer continues, "but it's Gotham" (Brubaker and Rucka, Gotham 125–126). This interest in the frustrations of individuals expected to make the right decision in midst of a demoralizing system propels Brubaker in his work within lesser known portions of the superhero universe.

Interested in exploring the world of Wildstorm (an independent super-hero publisher purchased by DC in 1999), Brubaker crafted *Point Blank*, a limited series based on an existing Wildstorm character. Although part of the defection of talent from mainstream superhero publishers (like Jim Lee, Wildstorm founder), the new publication company produced superhero titles mostly in line with grim gritty superhero aesthetic popular in the 1990s. With a light science fiction premise of erased memory, *Point Blank* looked at the way an individual (Grifter from *WildC.A.T.S.*) might literally work against himself and as a consequence never really know himself. The plot and themes of this series would set up a much more critically acclaimed series, to which Brubaker was extremely devoted: *Sleeper*. Although not as popular as some of his other efforts, it took its place alongside Wildstorm's *The Authority* and *Planetary* as one of the few truly subversive Wildstorm series that significantly revised superhero tropes (as Wildstorm's mission suggested their titles would). With Holden Carver, protagonist who worked undercover with brutal supervillains, the series undermines the expectations for justified violence associated with grim and gritty superhero stories by creating interesting, understandable villains; a reoccurring means of bonding among the villains would be sharing their origin stories. And with Holden's handler in a coma, no one knew that he was undercover and not in fact a traitor. Operating without a moral anchor in the other world from which he came,

Fig. 2: Holden Carver begins to appreciate Miss Misery's violence at an aesthetic level and without moral judgment against her in *Sleeper* Vol. 1, #3. (From *Sleeper* Vol. 1, #3 by Ed Brubaker and Sean Phillips © DC Comics; originally published by Wildstorm in 2003; available in *Sleeper: Out in the Cold*)

Holden recognized that their supposed moral ends often justified thoughts and actions as despicable as those of the criminal syndicate run by the super-intelligent villain known as Tao.

And as he cements his cover through a relationship with the syndicate operative called Miss Misery, he does so after developing an aesthetic appreciation for her sadistic acts (not unlike the reader's vicarious appreciation of supposedly justified acts of superhero violence in the grim and gritty era). Holden narrates, "[T]hat's when her true colors come out, while she's beating the living shit out of a guy too defeated to even resist. . . . In fact, she's never looked more beautiful than she does at that moment" (Brubaker, *The Sleeper* 180).

And later, Holden would reflect on that exact moment for Miss Misery and say, "I saw pure evil. And Jesus Fucking Christ, it was so beautiful" (209). Whether or not his words were carefully constructed for her sake, Holden finds the distinction between good and evil to be increasingly facile; as Tao argues, "You can kill on the orders of the USA, and tell yourself that you're still a really good person inside. . . . The road to hell is paved with good intentions. . . . So maybe it's time to stop lying to yourself about the intentions making any difference" (397–98). Like others in Tao's organization, Holden is valuable in part because he is superpowered, in his case not able to feel pain but able to externalize what would have been pain as blasts of energy. Of course, this numbness is descriptive of his condition as a whole, unable to feel anything by virtue of a lack of contrast with pain, and he becomes a heartless source of pain and suffering. After his handler returns to the scene and offers him a way out of the syndicate and a cure for his condition, Holden seems to realize that the reason he takes down Tao has as much to do with personal resentment as it does with the concept of justice now almost completely obscure to him. Working again with Sean Phillips, the general style is suitably dark for a superhero crime story. However, the most remarkable continuing motif is the jigsaw-type structure of panels on the page that do not always fill up the rectangular grid of the page and featuring negative space often filled with another image. Consequently, nothing seems to have absolute meaning in isolation, in its own terms, separate from its complicated context.

In 2004, Brubaker would no longer be limited by an exclusive contract with DC; encouraged by his friend and fellow crime writer, Brian Michael Bendis (Sava), Brubaker would begin a long relationship with Marvel as writer for the superhero title on which he would spend the most time: *Captain America*. While the title may have seemed out-of-line with Brubaker's subversive themes, Captain America quickly became more of an espionage thriller in line with sources such as *The Manchurian Candidate* and *Smiley's People*. While Brubaker maintained Captain America's man-out-of-time moral struggles, he used the espionage focus to recast Captain America's story and subvert expectations for the standard superhero story. In addition to more clearly portraying Captain America and Bucky as soldiers who killed when necessary, he regularly depicted the horrors of the "just war" of WWII (not allowing Captain America to feel too nostalgic for past times); in *Captain America and Bucky*, during the rescue of a POW, Bucky found a concentration camp with hundreds dead and with no means to rescue the survivors. In fact, Brubaker established his intention to play with the conventions of the superhero story in the very first issue of his run on the series. Captain America's archenemy, the Red Skull, reappears with the cosmic cube, and the issue is structured in part around his bombastic rhetoric concerning their enduring conflict and the devastation he will cause; however, this set-up is ultimately deflated as the Red Skull is shot by the single bullet of a secret assassin and revealed as dead in the final panel. Although his first, very popular arc would seem like business as usual in a superhero story (a controversial retcon bringing a dead hero back to life), the rebirth of Bucky Barnes as the Winter Soldier becomes a significant new way for Captain America to reconsider his mission and ethics. With the spy story convention of the brainwashed Soviet sleeper agent robbed of his identity, Captain America has a new reason to feel guilty about Bucky and resent any government committed to cover-up for its own sake.

As Joseph J. Darowski surveys in "The Superhero Narrative and the Graphic Novel," superhero stories are consistently updated but leave residual traces of the past, and essence of the superhero often requires the repetition described by Umberto Eco in his essay on Superman (13–14). Ironically, Brubaker engaged in this sort of repetition with a greatest hits tour of villains and past plot lines thanks to the "major change" wrought by Bucky's revival. In addition, Brubaker demonstrated a clear interest in the mythology of Captain America as a superhero even though he portrayed the mythology as culturally constructed. Undermining the myth of the American superhero as described by Robert Shelton and John Shelton Lawrence, Brubaker's version of Steve Rogers isn't inherently predisposed to be an authoritarian leader of his country. Instead, he responds to social pressures and lives up to expectations for the all-American hero but ultimately finds that the evil against which he's supposed to fight is often changing in an antidemocratic, superspy world. Brubaker lived up to expectations in terms that suited him such as those defined by comics scholar Charles Hatfield in his discussion of Jack Kirby and "the Marvel aesthetic": "Marvel's approach to superheroes

Fig. 3: An aerial perspective is used to add significance to the dramatic (albeit temporary) death of Captain America in *Captain America* Vol. 5, #25. (From *Captain America* Vol. 5, #25 by Ed Brubaker and Steve Epting © Marvel; originally published by Marvel in 2007; available in *The Death of Captain America: The Complete Collection*)

became more complex, less settled. . . . Good and evil forces were paired in a Manichean struggle in which victory of the good, though expected and hoped for at the end of each tale, turned out to be temporary, provisory, and fragile. Conflict reigned. The heroes' omnipotence was not guaranteed . . ." (Hatfield 137). As in the case of most spy thrillers, anxiety is ever present as anyone could betray you (Steve Roger's lover, Sharon Carter, while pregnant with his child, was programmed to kill Steve as Captain America). Despite the monstrous appearance of villains like the Red Skull, Arnim Zola, and Baron Zemo, Brubaker often crafted plots focused on how potentially similar the heroes are to the villains (with a focus on characters like the racist, hyperviolent 1950s Captain America). This type of mirroring would be represented in the artwork, especially with covers depicting Captain America and the Winter Soldier respectively as an American and Soviet agent. Thanks to his run on *Captain America*, Brubaker would become well known outside the comic book reading world with the death of Steve Rogers as Captain America in 2007, a comic book event that received international press coverage.

While most superhero fans knew that Steve Rogers would eventually return, the death is more than a publicity-driven nonevent as Brubaker uses it to skillfully explore a country living without its iconic (if invented) center. As an analysis of the hero worship that cultural critics often suggest threatens democratic ideals, this move was an extension of Brubaker's examination of the problems with America's image of itself especially as Bucky became Captain America. Of course, neither Captain America nor the Red Skull would stay dead, but neither return seemed to be a cheap response to fan pressure; in fact, the device enabling Captain America's revival would make a clear allusion to Kurt Vonnegut's *Slaughterhouse-Five* (a classic in science fiction rejecting a simplistic just war ideology).

As he continued his work on *Captain America*, Brubaker would also work on many other major Marvel properties including the X-Men, Dr. Doom, and the Immortal Iron Fist; most notably, he would take the reins from his friend Brian Michael Bendis on Marvel's most famous superhero crime title: *Daredevil*. Of course, the series would become known as a superhero story written like a crime novel after Frank Miller's tenure, deconstructing the superhero story and resuscitating the crime story in comics at the same time. With Bendis being the only writer who most fans felt equaled Miller in his gritty approach, Brubaker began the series with the difficult job of covering uncharted territory for this superhero who now had a publically known secret identity and was in prison for his vigilante activities. Further developing Daredevil's blindness as a metaphor, he makes Matt Murdock into one of the most self-deceiving, lonely, and angry characters in contemporary superhero comics. In prison, he does things he feels he never would on the outside, making alliance with hated enemies like the Kingpin and resorting to extreme measures to extract information from threats like Hammerhead; as he attacks, he narrates, "I know places where a sharp blow can paralyze a man. Or make him feel like his body is on fire . . . and his eyes are hot coals inside his head. It's the kind of move Daredevil usually avoids . . . it's torture. And I could make it so he can't scream . . . but I need him to talk" (Brubaker, *Daredevil: The Devil* 62). By referring to Daredevil in the third person, the fractured nature of Matt Murdock's identity becomes more apparent with this other more pragmatic identity presenting itself. Michael Lark again handles art for this superhero noir and symbolically obscures Daredevil's features with dark shadows more often than he reveals them. When Daredevil is cleared of the charges against him, the plot seems to have the potential to do what superhero comics do so well and return to the previously established status quo. However, this works as a ruse and as villains target people in his private life, Daredevil lashes out with the type of anger associated with a Jim Thompson protagonist. In reference to his work at Marvel, Brubaker states, "It's better to get a reaction from people. It's better to do the kind of stories that you'd actually like to read than to just worry too much and be too precious about the properties. What's interesting about the Marvel characters is that they were created to be broken" (Rahner). Using the crime subgenre of the prison drama as the ultimate metaphor for his run on the series, Brubaker portrays Daredevil not just as a vigilante hero but as a man conditioned by the system so that life in the "real" world of superheroism no longer makes sense to him. Eventually, he becomes the head of the league of typically villainous assassins known as the Hand and ironically, he finds peace as he descends the steps to their inner sanctum: "I think about all the mistakes I've made . . . all the friends I've caused so much pain . . . And I know I deserve whatever awaits me below . . . yet I pray I have the strength to endure it anyway. And then I smile . . . because I honestly can't remember the last time I prayed" (Brubaker, *Daredevil: Return of the King* 132–33). The complexity of the existential quandary produced by the blind corners of his identity is no less impressive than Brubaker's ability to maintain reader interest in and sympathy with an increasingly despicable character.

BEATING THE SYSTEM AND LOVING THE WRONG WOMAN

One of the most important events in Brubaker's career would be the launch of *Criminal* in 2006 as it serves as an integration of many of his preoccupations (pulp fiction tempered by human drama, traditional realism accentuated by revolutionary form). In addition, Brubaker would begin to critically analyze the history of his influences more directly within his creative work while he gradually distanced himself from company-owned properties, focusing more on his original creations. Published by Marvel but under the creator-owned

Icon imprint, *Criminal* was a series of limited series with all the stories drawn from different points in the history of the fictional Center City; this framework immediately invited comparisons to the most well-known crime series in the modern era of comics: Frank Miller's *Sin City*. While Brubaker was certainly part of the second-generation resurgence of crime comics also identified with Brian Michael Bendis (*Torso*) and Brian Azzarello (*100 Bullets*), modern crime comics owed its initial foothold in the new comics marketplace to *Sin City*. And yet, it would be with *Criminal* that Brubaker would begin to more clearly distance himself from Miller as an artistic influence: "I always joke that it's like *Sin City*, except that if someone jumped off a roof and landed on a car they'd die . . . and so would the people in the car. It's a more realistic version of that kind of thing. But it's more than that. *Sin City* was about taking the superhero conventions and putting them in a noir world. The capes were overcoats, basically. But what we're doing is creating our own world of noir and crime and exploring any kind of genre you can do within that field" (Phegley, "Ed Brubaker").

In *Criminal*'s first arc, "Coward," the focus is much more humanist and realistic, following Leo Patterson, a scam artist who struggles to care for Ivan, a scam artist mentor suffering from Alzheimer's disease. Leo is the "coward" of the title, perceived as such by others but in fact, too smart as a con man to engage in self-defeating violence with men motivated by the excessively masculine aesthetic of the world of criminals and crime fiction. When he backs down and diffuses a situation with men trying to intimidate his new girlfriend (an insider on a job gone wrong), she recognizes that he was not afraid of them: "[I backed down] because I'm afraid of other things . . . I guess. Violence just . . . It's got a ripple effect. You know that. And I try not to cause ripples. My ego can take a few morons thinking they scared me" (Brubaker, *Criminal: Coward* 71). In reference to crime conventions in "Coward," Brubaker states, "There's reader expectation with any sort of genre trope or cliché, so you can actually play off that expectation by sort of twisting the clichés in different directions. That's one of the main things that I wanted to do with this book and why I wanted to do this book" (Richards). However, while *Sin City* tends to engage and nearly parody crime fiction with its over-the-top representation of it, *Criminal* tends to subvert it in a way more subtle by providing stock characters with genuine motivations. Both employing and subverting standard conventions of crime fiction and film noir, Brubaker's work with Sean Phillips is very sophisticated with page layouts slowing the pace of the action story and panel arrangements representing the fractured perspective of Leo's misunderstood and uncertain self.

While "Coward was what Brubaker called an ultimate crime story (combining the con, the heist gone wrong, and the revenge story with a messy end) (Richards), the next story, "Lawless," demonstrates how numerous and extensive the world of crime fiction conventions are: an AWOL Tracy Lawless tries to find his brother's murderer by becoming involved with his brother's criminal enterprises and falling for his brother's lover. Also, the following three *Criminal* short stories (collected as "The Dead and the Dying") would make references to plot devices from several Blaxploitation films and visual allusions to the film *Chinatown* and a famous Johnny Craig illustration in *Crime Suspenstories*, among many others. Making a fan favorite character with soldier-turned-criminal the protagonist of "Lawless" (later reappearing in "The Sinners" arc), this story depicts Lawless following in his father's footsteps and demonstrates Brubaker's enduring interest in twinning mentioned earlier in connection with his superhero work. However, his interest in twinning has less to do with the likenesses between hero and villain in the Manichean battle between good and evil. Instead, he presents it almost as an exposé on the illusion of the unique self, the ability to escape repetition (famously seen in crime fiction like *The Maltese Falcon* with Sam Spade's description of a man who started his life over only to live an incredibly similar life). This exploration of twinning would be seen more overtly in the creator-owned series written at roughly the same time and also published by Icon: *Incognito*. A supervillain is placed in witness protection and is forced to live an ordinary life until he discovers that recreational drugs allow him to work past the inhibitions authorities placed on his superpowers. With few options open to him, he puts on a mask to fight crime, anxious to do violence for some reason even if it has to be the "right" reason. Before witness protection, he works with his twin who was killed in action, and throughout the course of the story, he learns he is a genetic offshoot of a famous Shadow-like superhero of the past. In addition, when his activities cause him to be discovered, he is recruited by the authorities as bait and hunted by a psychotic genetic double. While again exploring some of the themes in *Sleeper*, *Incognito* is more about the question of one's ability to escape patterns already established (regardless of how one's behavior is characterized).

In addition, as *Incognito* continues this focus on noir in a philosophical way, it makes noir more particular with an interest in comic book characters of the pulp era: "It's kind of apocalyptic noir in this weird way. Noir isn't really a genre—People think of it as a genre, but the people who think of it as that, when they start to tell you what movies that would fit into that, don't realize how elastic that actually is. . . . It's kind of an experiment to take pulp and make up sort of an evolution of where these pulp-styled characters would have gone and how they would have affected a world . . . and to also try to tell it through this really character-driven noir story" (Mautner). This interest in pulp traditions began in a literal way with Brubaker's decision for single issues of *Criminal* to include extra material such as essays on crime fiction and film; in addition to evoking the grab bag feel of pulp fiction magazine anthologies, these extras were not included in the collected trade paperbacks (working against the general trend of encouraging the purchase of the respectable version of the comic book known as the graphic novel collection). Likewise and perhaps more significantly, *Incognito* included essays on pulp characters by comic historian Jess Nevins not reprinted in the collections; these essays become explorations of this idea of pulp traditions that never continued with Nevins eventually blending real history with fiction of the Zeppelin Pulps (featuring the characters wholly imagined by Brubaker for *Incognito*).

As Brubaker moved more into the anti-institutional world with his themes and his time spent with his creator-owned work, an unexpected controversy emerged in association with his work with Captain America in 2010. In a crowd scene with protesters characterized by the Falcon as white and racist, letterer Joe Caramanga filled an empty protest sign with a slogan alluding to the Tea Party: "Tea bag the libs before they tea bag you!" Even though he explained that he was not responsible for the slogan and that Marvel would change it for the trade paperback, he nevertheless resented the excessive reaction directed toward him: "I was getting death threats for two panels of a comic book. How is that not like the Taliban or al-Qaeda? So that really shocked me" (Sava). Regardless of his openly left-of-center politics, he had new reason to feel angry with the pressure of the powerful unwilling to dialogue within systemic structures. At roughly the same time, Brubaker would develop "The Last of the Innocent" arc of *Criminal*, a critique of the system of the comics industry and the larger culture that is not strident or angry but rather nuanced and personal. This metafictive work (a comic about comics) was something set up at the start of *Criminal* with Leo Patterson reading a comic strip featuring "Frank Kafka," a private investigator who visually evokes Dick Tracy and whose name alludes to the existential puzzles of Franz Kafka's fiction; as Leo states about the crime series, "It never makes any God damned sense." With 2008's "Bad Night," the series began more obviously to reinterpret the meaning of crime comics in American history and the faulty assumptions that have placed comic books in their position as kids' stuff in American culture. In "Bad Night," Jacob is the insomniac writer of the *Frank Kafka PI* comic strip; as Jacob is drawn back into a life of crime, the angular, black and grey Frank Kafka literally appears within panels also featuring Jacob as a stylistic contrast to Sean Phillips's gritty rendering of Jacob's "real" noir world. When Frank Kafka first appears in the story, it is easy for a reader to assume that the private investigator is a subconscious coping mechanism used by the protagonist, but Jacob actually doesn't interact with him until much later in the story. Consequently, the early appearances have as much potential to be read as part of a cultural subconscious in which the reader participates. As a Dick Tracy lookalike, Frank Kafka has a superficially benign presence, but as he encourages Jacob's violent behavior, he is more accurately understood as a ruthless representation of a culture's repressed anger.

The use of multiple artistic styles to evoke different comic book associations continues with the "The Last of the Innocent," the *Criminal* story whose title refers to the most famous American book of comics criticism: Fredric Wertham's *Seduction of the Innocent*. The aforementioned nuance of this work as a commentary on this often resented and oversimplified period in comics history is fairly remarkable considering some of the reasons Brubaker may have had to resent the limitations of the systems around him in 2010. Although a complex work with an approach that could be characterized as postmodern, "The Last of the Innocent" was a deeply personal, perhaps autobiographical work, conceived while Brubaker's father was dying: "I was sort of wallowing in that childhood nostalgia a lot. And then this story just kind of appeared to me. Like, what if I did a story about these characters from this made-up, analogue version of a kid's comic, who all grew up? But they grew up fucked-up, because they grew up exactly like Dr. Wertham's worst fears of what kids reading comics would be. . . . So I wanted to do something that approached nostalgia in a crime story" (Sava). Brubaker portrays Riley Richards as a down-on-his-luck gambler who longs for the life of his youth before he was married and therefore decides to murder his wife. With even more artistic flair than that seen in "Bad Night," the flashbacks to Riley's earlier life would be represented in an artistic style in contrast to Phillips's moody realism, an artistic style much like that of *Archie* comics. Of course, teen humor comics would represent what Fredric Wertham, author of *Seduction of the Innocent*, considered safe as he campaigned against crime comics in the 1950s (with the hometown of Archie Andrews representing an idyllic version of what America should be in the estimation of those who wanted to enforce a certain modicum of control). As comic scholar Amy Nyberg states, "The major factor in the success of the campaign against [crime] comics was linkage of comics book reading to juvenile delinquency, a problem representing the ultimate loss of social control over children" (Nyberg ix). However, in "Last of the Innocent," this *Archie*-shaped, rose-colored notion of the past not only motivates Riley to commit murder—killing his wife with an injury to the eye, what Wertham especially dreaded; it also turns out to be anything but safe and secure. Within the *Archie* world that represented Riley's past, he cheats on the girl next door, his friend becomes addicted to drugs, and multiple murders are committed to hide a single crime in his small town. Rather than make a frontal assault against Wertham, the work challenges the myth of the prelapsarian past motivating overzealous reformers such as Wertham; in turn, "The Last of the Innocent" works as a commentary on itself, crime comics in general, and American culture as a whole.

If anything, Brubaker makes a case for the crime comics writers of the 1950s as they are characterized by David Hajdu in *The Ten-Cent Plague*: "[T] hey were . . . . cultural insurgents. They expressed in their lurid panels, thereby helping to instill in their readers, a disregard for the niceties of proper society, a passion for wild ideas and fast action, a cynicism toward authority of all sorts, and a tolerance, if not an appetite, for images of prurience and violence" (Hajdu 330). And yet while this is the case, the story doesn't function only as a work of cultural criticism that acknowledges human desire; the story is also the tragedy of an individual who doesn't know himself and is swallowed by the indistinct boundaries of character provided by his nostalgia; he embraces that unknowing. In order to have an alibi for the murder he commits, Riley takes his former best friend (a Jughead Jones lookalike) on a bender and causes his friend's relapse into substance abuse. When he later protects himself by financially destroying his suspicious father-in-law and setting up his friend's overdose, Riley finds his peace. However, it means losing any sense of the truth of fallen world around him: "There's a dull pain in my stomach. A heartsickness, I guess. But it feels like a new beginning, too. Like I'm finally safe. Because the last person—maybe the only person—who really knew me . . . is lying on a slab in the Brookview county morgue. So now I can be whoever I want" (Brubaker, *Criminal: The Last* 103). Riley allows the desire that re-created the past that never existed to recharacterize the loss of his one true friend as a positive thing. In addition, over the series of panels in which this monologue unfolds, the representation of Riley and his recently reclaimed hometown girlfriend become less realistic and more iconographic like renderings in Archie comics; and at the end, with "So now I can be whoever I want," they are essentially Archie and Betty but set against (and oblivious to) the run-down backdrop where a drug deal goes down.

And even more recently, Brubaker, again with Sean Phillips, continues to stretch the boundaries of genre with *Fatale* (2012), his noir turned epic horror series that successfully mines the common ground between genres and crafts noir as a transhistorical phenomenon. After he attends the funeral of pulp fiction writer Dominic Raines (his father's best friend), Nicolas Lash receives an inheritance from Raines: an unpublished novel that is more sophisticated and stranger than anything else in Raines body of work. Shortly thereafter, he's attacked by men wearing bowler hats and is saved by Josephine, a seductive woman he met at the funeral. Symbolically emasculated by losing his leg in the car wreck that ended the rescue, he begins his obsessive search for Josephine and that includes reading the novel; despite its supernatural elements, the novel tells the story of a character that could be a young version of Raines and the seductress in the novel has strange resemblances to Josephine (or Jo, as many know her). The juxtaposition of Nicolas's story alongside that of the novel is one of the subtle complexities of the early part of the run as it's unclear how the reader should understand the story of young Hank Raines: a writer's fantasy, a reimagining of the novel, or a flashback to a past time. According to the story, Jo was apparently given her ability to seduce men and stay young by an occult ceremony performed by a Satanic cult led by a monstrous figure in human guise. Although the first collected edition of *Fatale* offered a back cover blurb that tried to craft it as the story of Nicolas, it really is the story of Josephine and that is what makes the story notable. The title refers to the femme fatale, one of the most well-known conventions of noir—more of a convention than a character. With a Freudian reading of woman as the problem, noir often depicts a woman who seduces a man and convinces him to commit a crime (with the ultimate intention of using and betraying the man); the femme fatale is more a force of the oppressive systems of the noir world than a real person, an emblem of selfish desire seeking to coopt the individual will of male protagonists. However, *Fatale* makes Jo an understandable and sympathetic character infused with a sense of tragedy as she tries to deal with the "curse" of her condition.

And as the series continues, the story of her long life becomes more complex with the initial structure left behind and the story of Jo's development as a sympathetic character taking center stage. Brubaker describes part of the rationale behind extending Jo's story from a twelve-issue series into a twenty-four-issue series in this way: "I just love structure—I'm such a slave to my own structure sometimes—I really needed some other way to do it. One of my favorite writers is Milan Kundera. I've always loved how he writes his novels in sections. Sometimes there will be a whole section that doesn't really seem to relate to the other parts of the book at all. And I thought, eh, fuck it, I'll just do a third arc that's just four short stories that reveal little bits and pieces of Jo's history and of the deeper mystery behind the curse—while also hopefully being fun, little horror stories" (Rozeman). The cynical reading of doubling the length of the series is that the producer wanted to further capitalize on its popularity and sell more copies of the issues, trades, and omnibuses. While that may have been a pronounced interest for Image as publisher, Brubaker and Phillips are not at a point in their careers where they need the money from twelve extra issues. Like *Criminal* and *Incognito* before, *Fatale* included essays on noir, pulp, and history in each issues (some again by Jess Nevins) not to be reprinted in the collected versions. With this in mind, the decision to extend the series seems to be a choice tied to the traditional production of comic books, a serially produced medium that encourages a type of storytelling beyond the ideas of unity associated with the classic novel. Also, as Brubaker's run on *Winter Soldier* came to an end, he moved into a time in his career where he was only working on original creations like *Fatale* and indicated no intention to write anything other than creator-owned material. Brubaker states, "I never planned on doing superhero comics for as long as I did. I was having a really good time and making a really good living doing it. And it was really creatively fulfilling, but now I feel like the more creatively fulfilling thing I'm doing is *Fatale* and some other stuff I've got planned. I like having complete control. I wasn't so much trying to make a huge statement it ended up coming out as. But I'm fine with it becoming this huge thing. More people need to be reminded that you can do this" (Phegley, "Brubaker Drives"). With espionage stories like *Velvet* and crime stories like *The Fade Out* (both published by Image), Brubaker continues to remind people that this can be done. Thanks to their popularity and critical acclaim, Brubaker and Phillips have signed an exclusive contract with Image that not only maintains their ownership but also frees them from pitching their work and allows them approval on design and format (Johnston). And Brubaker's ability to capture an audience beyond the fanboys at the comic book store has increased with work on film versions of *Sleeper*, *Criminal*, and *Incognito*.

HOW THE CRIMINAL CAN BE CAUGHT

It's easy to identify Ed Brubaker as one of the most popular and significant creators of the generation that came to prominence during the direct market boom of the 1980s and 1990s. It's more difficult to trace how various parts of his career have fed the creative mind that consistently pushes boundaries while satisfying the fans and the critics. Initially propelled by the alternative

comics of direct market, Brubaker was obviously inspired by the new prominence of autobiography as a comics genre. That point of inspiration did not
disappear with the end of more obviously autobiographical works like *Lowlife*
but continued to propel some of works seemingly to be the least amenable to
such an approach like *Captain America* (with his uncle's work in the CIA) and
Criminal: The Last of the Innocent (with his father's death). One of his standard
devices is the first-person narrative, characteristic not only of the modern
novel but a pronounced part of crime fiction. This opportunity to articulate
the self is appealing to modern readers but represents a perspective subject
to bias, an unreliable way to gauge a wholly accurate sense of identity and
history. This sense of mystery at the intersection between autobiography and
crime fiction has the potential to lead to anxiety and dread (feelings experi-
enced by many of Brubaker's characters ranging from Catwoman to Holden
Carver, from Daredevil to Leo Patterson). And even the most loyal of friends
seem unable to provide a solution for this essential problem. Whether it is
S.H.I.E.L.D. in *Captain America* or the Hyde criminal syndicate in *Criminal:
Lawless*, Brubaker's works depict justifiable fears of dehumanizing systems
that are always likely to spin out of control. In short, Brubaker's characters
are often estranged from themselves and from each other.

And yet, while Brubaker appreciates and accentuates grim and gritty superhero stories that approach these issues in less refined ways, he also takes
their history seriously and does not aim to wholly deconstruct the superhero
mythos. Instead, he tends to strip heroes down to their historical origin point
as vigilantes against a corrupt system fighting for the least of these; in the
case of Captain America (particularly when Bucky Barnes assumes the role),
a symbol can have the power to transcend the weaknesses of an individual
and the limitations of the society that tries to coopt the symbol. At the same
time, he points out the problems with heroes approved by the public-at-large
and therefore become ruthless at upholding the rules that govern the system.
In reference to those not favored by the system, Brubaker's work regularly
demonstrates an interest in secondary characters and also delves into the
psychology of villains (while refusing to oversimplify and explain them) in
genre fiction that regularly employs type characters in order to drive the plot
toward another fetishized act of sex or violence. Brubaker elevates characters
who seem to be non-heroic and secondary into protagonists such as Charlie
in "An Accidental Death" or Jacob in *Criminal: Bad Night*; as is the case with
unrepentant Miss Misery in *Sleeper* and Zack Overkill in *Incognito*, he looks
directly into the dark corners of criminals' life without resorting to a moral
epiphany that leads to redemption. In short, Brubaker presents roundness

of characters and thereby argues at an aesthetic level for the importance of those least valued and most often dismissed by culture.

And in terms of aesthetics, Brubaker's sophisticated narrative layering simultaneously employs and undermines basic expectation placed upon his genres of choice. His interesting articulation of comic books in relation to culture has the medium straddling a line between pulp and art in a way that suggests certain theoretical approaches. He offers what should be understood as a poststructuralist refusal to distinguish low culture from high culture in sociological/historical paradigm. Concomitantly, he demonstrates a postmodernist tendency to move beyond the hegemonic control of cultural structures through metafiction. However, this intensely theoretical language is used to demonstrate what he does and yet what is only a secondary consequence of an approach that is less postmodernist and more humanist. In large part, Brubaker breaks down artistic and political barriers because he finds intersections between his genres of choice by means of situating them within a very personal story of the self in history. In short, his often profane, sexual, and hyperviolent stories are made into something far-reaching through his respectful treatment of human frailty. In Brubaker's estimation, frailty (sometimes tempered by a good decision) is what we have; consequently, base desires are considered alongside high ideals, and an honest depiction of things is his end goal. In his conclusion to "The Crime Narrative and the Graphic Novel," Rich Shivener suggests that the work of Brubaker and Phillips operates as part of an American cultural heritage and will have historical importance: "[C]rime comics still have a notable presence, thanks primarily to writer Ed Brubaker and artist Sean Phillips . . . the approaches of Brubaker and Phillips . . . will be remembered as crime narratives continue into the twenty-first century" (Shivener 37). A good endnote to be sure but in an introduction to *Criminal: Lawless*, Frank Miller writes something like a note to Brubaker that seems to encapsulate more of the way that Brubaker thinks about his own work: "Not many people understand what makes a crime story tick . . . the essential inner darkness that a good crime yarn exposes, relishes in. . . . Your stuff . . . doesn't snicker at what it is, and it doesn't apologize for it either" (Miller, "Introduction"). While Miller's motivation may be different from my own, I agree that Brubaker realizes the full potential of the pulp traditions that he loves. While his approach may be informed by complex art and ideas, he never sees them as separate from comics, pulp magazines, and crime fiction; and he never apologizes for his love of that stuff because he understands pulp traditions as vitally connected to the human experience.

My motivation as editor of this collection is that Brubaker is not only a smart guy who has produced some great work but also someone who has said some very interesting things about his work (and comics and its culture in general). The selections made are meant to represent a spread in terms of time and topic but some have been chosen for some very particular reasons that I'll mention here but with very little detail. (I'm working with the assumption that great detail is unnecessary since the point of an interview collection is to read the interviews.) Some interviews focus on "new" assignments/specific works at certain points in his career: Contino and Giles dealing with *Catwoman* (and *Batman*) and Mithra with *Daredevil*. Others focus on the moves between corporate and independent work in the Marvel/Icon era: Richards, Rahner, and Mautner. Others deal with Brubaker's ideas as a writer of comic books and sometimes also of film, television, and web series: Swiercynski, Cohen, and Hood. Others deal with his genre blending and advocacy of creator ownership: Phegley ("Brubaker Drives 'Fatale' . . ."), Rozeman, and Royal Nonesuch. And still others are more clearly trying to connect various aspects of his career and in some cases, serve as retrospectives: O'Shea, Phegley ("Crime, Superheroes . . ."), and Sava. Of course, it is unfair of me to pigeonhole the interviews in any absolute sense and these foci do not exclude other areas of discussion; in the end, all the conversations reveal different aspects of Brubaker's mind: creative, critical, witty, and humane.

I would like to thank all those who helped with this project in large and small ways. Thanks to all of the interviewers who did the work that made this volume possible, especially those who recognized Ed Brubaker as a major talent early in his career.

Thanks to those who encouraged me in the research necessary to put together a well-rounded collection, especially my fellow researchers at the Michigan State University Special Collections Library, the Judson University Benjamin P. Browne Library, and the Ida Fuller Hovey Public Library. Of course, thanks to Ed Brubaker for his work as a comics creator. Along those lines, thanks to Sean Phillips and Michael Lark (Ed's frequent partners in crime) and special thanks to Sean for the cover image. And as always, thanks to my wife Anna and my kids Bella, Ripley, Griffin, and Reuben for giving me a little more time in the criminal world I love so much.

TW

Works Cited

Bendis, Brian Michael. "Introduction." Ed Brubaker, Michael Lark, and Sean Phillips. *Scene of the Crime*. Image, 2012. Print. i–ii.

Benton, Mike. *Crime Comics: The Illustrated History*. Dallas: Taylor, 1993. Print.

Brubaker, Ed. *A Completer Lowlife*. Top Shelf, 2001. Print.

Brubaker, Ed, Marc Andreyko, and Chris Samnee. *Captain America and Bucky: The Story of Bucky Barnes*. New York: Marvel, 2012. Print.

Brubaker, Ed, Darwyn Cooke, and Brad Rader. *Catwoman: The Trail of the Catwoman*. DC, 2012. Print.

Brubaker, Ed, Steve Epting, and Michael Lark. *Captain America: Winter Soldier*. New York: Marvel, 2014. Print.

Brubaker, Ed, Steve Epting, Mike Perkins, and Jackson Guice. *The Death of Captain American: The Complete Collection*. New York: Marvel, 2013. Print.

Brubaker, Ed, Jackson Guice, and Luke Ross. *Captain America: Two Americas*. New York: Marvel, 2010. Print.

Brubaker, Ed, Bryan Hitch, and Jackson Guice. *Captain America Reborn*. New York: Marvel, 2010. Print.

Brubaker, Ed, and Michael Lark. *Daredevil: Inside and Out, Vol. 1*. New York: Marvel, 2011. Print.

———. *Daredevil: The Return of the King*. New York: Marvel, 2011. Print.

Brubaker, Ed, Michael Lark, and Sean Phillips. *Scene of the Crime*. Image, 2012. Print.

Brubaker, Ed, and Sean Phillips. *Criminal: Bad Night*. Icon, 2009. Print.

———. *Criminal: Coward*. Icon, 2007. Print.

———. *Criminal: Lawless*. Icon, 2007. Print.

———. *Criminal: The Dead and the Dying*. Icon, 2008. Print.

———. *Criminal: The Last of the Innocent*. Icon, 2011. Print.

———. *Fatale, Book 1: Death Chases Me*. Image, 2012. Print.

———. *Fatale, Book 2: The Devil's Business*. Image, 2013. Print.

———. *Incognito: The Classified Edition*. Icon, 2012. Print.

———. *The Sleeper Omnibus*. DC, 2013. Print.

Brubaker, Ed, and Eric Shanower. *An Accidental Death. Dark Horse Presents* 67. Milwaukie, OR: Dark Horse. Nov. 1992. Print. 22–31.

Contino, Jennifer M. "Cat Got Ed's Tongue." *Sequential Tart* 4.12 (Dec. 2001). Web.

Darowski, Joseph J. "The Superhero Narrative and the Graphic Novel." *Critical Insights: The Graphic Novel*. Ed. Gary Hoppenstand. Amenia, NY: Grey House, 2014. Print. 3–16.

Duncan, Randy, and Matthew J. Smith. *The Power of Comics: History, Form, and Culture*. New York: Bloomsbury, 2013. Print.

Giles, Keith. "Ed Brubaker Interview." *Comic Book Resources*. 17 Dec. 2001. Web. 14 May 2012.

Groth, Gary, and Tom Spurgeon. "'I Just Think of Myself as a Pulp Writer': The Ed Brubaker Interview." *Comics Journal* 263 (Oct./Nov. 2004). Print. 59–99.

Hajdu, David. *The Ten-Cent Plague: The Great Comic Book Scare and How It Changed America*. New York: Farrar, Straus, and Giroux, 2008. Print.

Hatfield, Charles. "Jack Kirby and the Marvel Aesthetic." *The Superhero Reader*. Eds. Charles Hatfield, Jeet Heer, and Kent Worchester. Jackson: UP of Mississippi, 2013. Print. 136–54.

Johnston, Rich. "Talking to Ed Brubaker on His Five Year Deal with Image, *The Fade Out*, and *The Winter Soldier*, at Image Expo." *Bleeding Cool*. 15 Jan. 2014. Web. 15 Feb. 2014.

Mautner, Chris. "An Interview with Ed Brubaker." *Patriot-News*. 12 Mar. 2009. Web. 14 May 2012.

Miller, Frank. "Introduction." Ed Brubaker and Sean Phillips. *Criminal: Lawless*. New York: Icon, 2007. Print. i.

Nyberg, Amy. *Seal of Approval: The History of the Comics Code*. Jackson: UP of Mississippi, 1998. Print.

O'Shea, Tim. "An ORCA Q&A with Ed Brubaker." *The Comic Book Electronic Magazine*. 30 May 2003. Web. 22 Nov. 2013.

Phegley, Kiel. "Brubaker Drives 'Fatale' into a Creator-Owned Career." *Comic Book Resources*. 17 Aug. 2012. Web. 17 Nov. 2013.

——. "Ed Brubaker: Crime, Superheroes, and Comic Book History." *Publishers Weekly*. 15 Sep. 2009. Web. 14 May 2012.

Rahner, Mark. "Brubaker's Noir World." *Seattle Times*. 4 Oct. 2006. Web. 20 Nov. 2013.

Richards, Dave. "The Right to Remain Violent: Brubaker Talks 'Criminal.'" *Comic Book Resources*. 3 Oct. 2006. Web. 14 May, 2012.

Rozeman, Mark. "Catching Up with *Fatale* Writer Ed Brubaker." *Paste*. 16 Apr. 2013. Web. 17 Nov. 2013.

Sava, Oliver. "Interview: Ed Brubaker." *The Onion AV Club*. 20 July 2011. Web. 14 May 2012.

Shivener, Rich. "The Crime Narrative and the Graphic Novel." *Critical Insights: The Graphic Novel*. Ed. Gary Hoppenstand. Amenia, NY: Grey House, 2014. Print. 29–40.

Wright, Bradford. *Comic Book Nation: The Transformation of Youth Culture in America*. Baltimore: Johns Hopkins UP, 2001. Print.

CHRONOLOGY

1966   Born October 17 in a naval hospital in Maryland; named after his Uncle Ed, a CIA intelligence officer; lives with grandmother in Martinsburg, West Virginia.

1968   Father, a naval intelligence officer, returns from Vietnam; moves to Sterling Park, Virginia.

1970   Moves to the US Naval Station in Guantanamo Bay, Cuba; begins reading some of father's comic book collection including *The Fantastic Four*, *The Hulk*, *Captain America*, and EC crime comics.

1972   Attends school at the Guantanamo Bay Naval Base.

1973   Moves to San Diego, California.

1974   Parents divorce.

1975   Writes and draws first comics with friends.

1980   Mother remarries; lives with father in Hawaii.

1981   Begins reading more independent comics (*Epic Magazine*, *Cerebus*, and *The Comics Journal*).

1983   Meets the Hernandez brothers at a comic convention.

1984   Works at Comic Kingdom in San Diego, California.

1987   Draws a portion of *Gumby 3-D* published by Blackthorne; writes and draws *Pajama Chronicles* published by Blackthorne, canceled after one issue.

1989   Moves to San Francisco, California; writes and draws *Purgatory USA* published by Slave Labor.

1991   Writes and draws *Lowlife* published by Slave Labor (and later by Caliber); begins contributing to *Dark Horse Presents*; writes "Burning Man" (drawn by Mike Christian) for *Dark Horse Presents* #50.

1992   Edits *Monkey Wrench* published by Caliber; writes "An Accidental Death" (drawn by Eric Shanower) for *Dark Horse Presents* #65–67.

1993   Nominated for Eisner award for best writer/artist team ("An Accidental Death").

1995   Writes "Here and Now" in *Dark Horse Presents* #96–98 and "Bird

Dog" in *Dark Horse Presents* #100; writes *Prez: Smells Like Teen President* (drawn by Eric Shanower) published by Vertigo (with Prez created by Joe Simon, his first work with a company-owned character).

1997   Writes and draws *At the Seams* one-off published by Alternative Comics; nominated for Ignatz Award for Best Graphic Novel (*At the Seams*).

1998   Writes and draws *Detour* published by Alternative Comics, canceled after one issue; earns Harvey Award nomination for best new series (*Detour*).

1999   Writes *Scene of the Crime* (drawn by Michael Lark and Sean Phillips) published by Vertigo; becomes engaged to Melanie Tomlin, an independent filmmaker, some time after bonding over shared opinion of *Planet of the Apes*; gives first major interview to Gary Groth (interview later completed by Tom Spurgeon and published in *The Comics Journal* in 2004).

2000   Begins one-year exclusive contract with DC Comics; writes *Batman* (drawn by Scott McDaniel) published by DC (2000–2002); writes *Deadenders* (drawn by Warren Pleece) published by Vertigo (2000–2001); marries Melanie Tomlin; nominated for Eisner award for Best Writer (*Scene of the Crime*).

2001   Writes backup stories in *Detective Comics* published by DC, including "Trail of the Catwoman," (drawn by Darwyn Cooke) leading to ongoing *Catwoman* series (2001–2005); writes *The Sandman Presents: The Dead Boy Detectives* (drawn by John Totleben), a spin-off with Neil Gaiman–created characters, published by Vertigo; *The Fall*, previously published in *Dark Horse Presents*, is published in *Drawn and Quarterly*.

2002   Writes "Death Wish for Two" with Geoff Johns (drawn by Scott McDaniel) for *Batman* #606–607 published by DC; writes *Point Blank* (drawn by Sean Phillips) published by Wildstorm, leading directly into *Sleeper*.

2003   Writes *Detective Comics* #777–786 published by DC Comics; writes *Sleeper* (drawn by Sean Phillips) published by Wildstorm (2003–2005); writes *Gotham Central* (co-written by Greg Rucka and drawn by Michael Lark) published by DC Comics (2003–2006); writes *The Authority* (drawn by Jim Lee and then Dustin Nguyen) published by Wildstorm; conducts arm wrestling contest at Isotope comics to promote *Sleeper* with signed copies of the comic as awards for winners; nominated for Eisner award for Best Writer (*Catwoman*,

Detective Comics, Gotham Central); wins Prism Award for "Disguises" in *Catwoman*.

2004   Nominated for Eisner award for Best Writer (*Catwoman, Detective Comics, Gotham Central, Sleeper*); Wins GLAAD Media Award for *Catwoman*.

2005   Begins exclusive contract with Marvel; Writes *Captain America* (drawn by Steve Epting) published by Marvel (2005–2012), introducing Bucky Barnes as the Winter Soldier.

2006   Writes *Daredevil* (drawn by Michael Lark) (2006–2009), *The Immortal Iron Fist* (co-written with Matt Fraction and drawn by David Aja) (2006–2008), *Books of Doom* (drawn by Pablo Raimondi), and *X-Men Deadly Genesis* (drawn by Trevor Harisine) published by Marvel; writes the first volume of *Criminal* (drawn by Sean Phillips) published by Icon Comics(2006–2011), Marvel's creator-owned imprint; wins Harvey Award for Best Writer (*Captain America*).

2007   Captain America assassinated; nominated for Eisner Award for Best Continuing Series (*Captain America, Daredevil*); wins Eisner Award for Best Writer (*Captain America, Daredevil*, and *Criminal*) and for Best New Series (*Criminal*); wins Harvey award for Best Writer (*Daredevil*).

2008   Writes *Incognito* (drawn by Sean Phillips) published by Icon Comics (2008–2011); Sam Raimi's Star Roads Entertainment options *Sleeper* as film project; wins Eisner Award for Best Writer (*Captain America, Criminal, Daredevil, The Immortal Iron Fist*).

2009   *Captain America: Reborn* published; writes screenplay for *Angel of Death* web series (starring Zoe Bell and Lucy Lawless), premiering on Crackle (distributed by Sony Picture Television); writes screenplay for episode of *Batman: Black and White*.

2010   Writes *Secret Avengers* (drawn by Mike Deodato) published by Marvel; *Captain America* #602 causes controversy with its depiction of Tea Party protestors; 20th Century Fox options *Incognito* as film project; nominated for Eisner Award for Best Limited Series (*Incognito*); wins Eisner award for Best Writer (*Captain America, Criminal, Daredevil, Incognito, Marvels Project*).

2011   Writes screenplay for *Criminal: Coward* with David Slade set to direct film for Hunting Lane Films; wins award at International Noir Festival in Lyon for Best Crime Comic (*Criminal: The Sinners*).

2012   Ends run on *Captain* America and begins *Winter Soldier* (drawn by Butch Guice) published by Marvel; writes *Fatale* (drawn by Sean

Phillips) published by Image Comics (2012–2014); writes television pilots for Fox ("Rising Suns") and NBC (untitled espionage thriller); Marvel Studios announces that the second Captain America film will be based on Brubaker's Winter Soldier story (causing Brubaker to tweet "Holy Shit"); wins Eisner Award for Best Limited Series (*Criminal: Last of the Innocent*).

2013   Writes *Velvet* (drawn by Steve Epting) published by Image; Matt Damon and Ben Affleck to produce *Sleeper* as a film with a script to be written by Sean Ryan and David Wiener.

2014   Begins exclusive contract with Image; writes *The Fade Out* (drawn by Sean Phillips) published by Image; makes cameo appearance in film version of *Captain America: The Winter Soldier* as the Winter's Soldier's handler.

ED BRUBAKER: CONVERSATIONS

Cat Got Ed's Tongue

JENNIFER M. CONTINO / 2001

Originally published in *Sequential Tart* (4.12) December 2001. Web. Reprinted by permission. www.sequentialtart.com.

Ed Brubaker's responsible for the new life that a certain cat is enjoying right now. The Catwoman has returned and Brubaker is at the helm, scribing her latest adventures. Over the past ten years many of today's hottest writers have taken a turn on the feline fatale and a lot of fans are anxious to see how Brubaker's run will be different. Lately, he has been involved in many different projects, but we just wanted to learn as much as possible about his take on Selina Kyle.

Sequential Tart: Do you like cats?
Ed Brubaker: Yes, we have two cats. I like cats, and always have, because they are, for the most part, worry free pets. If you feed them, and clean their box, they're happy. They aren't constantly after you for attention. Plus, they have class. They just want to chill on the couch and not be bothered.

ST: Who is Catwoman?
EB: You're kidding, right?

ST: Well . . . there might be some independent comics fans who've never read a four-color book and don't know a thing about her.
EB: Oh, you're not kidding . . . Shit. Okay, well, Catwoman is Selina Kyle, a long time Batman nemesis who has gone through a lot of different incarnations since 1940 or so. Originally she actually had this horrific Cathead mask, which we show on the first splash page in the background, sort of. In my version, Selina Kyle follows the path that Frank Miller laid out and hinted at in *Batman Year One*, so long ago. She's a girl whose parents died when she

was young and she and her sister were sent away to orphanages and youth authority type places. From the time she was about fifteen, Selina survived on the streets, and learned to despise a lot of the world around her. When she witnessed Batman's early career, it inspired her to become Catwoman, who was basically a thief and a hellraiser. She's been a lot of things over the years since then, and some have worked, others not so much. So I'm trying to find a clear path to have her follow, and bring her back to her roots to some degree.

ST: What makes her different from the average Batman villain?
EB: Well, for one thing, she's been able to carry her own comic for almost ten years. But I guess the main difference is that she isn't such a cut and dried villain. She's just not totally in favor of Law and Order, because she's seen the hypocrisy in the system at work too often.

ST: Catwoman's been around for over sixty years in one form or another, how will your version of her be different from the rest?
EB: Smaller breasts.

ST: What's your opinion on comics continuity? How much attention to continuity will you be paying as far as this series goes?
EB: Actually, I think continuity is one of the biggest problems of mainstream comics. At least, cross-universe-continuity. Whenever you have to acknowledge what else is happening in other comic books, it becomes constricting in some way or another. I think it's hard enough to keep the continuity straight in one book at a time, honestly, which the eight-year run of the previous edition of *Catwoman* is ample proof of. As far as continuity in this book goes, I'm trying to have it stand on its own as much as humanly possible, so a casual reader could pick it up and understand it easily. This series is very self-contained. I don't plan any crossovers with *Batman* (the comic) though the character will appear occasionally. I'm really just trying to build a series around my characters that will be engaging on its own, so if it's the only DC book you read, you won't feel like you're missing some huge pieces anywhere. I think all comics should be that way to a larger degree.

ST: In the *Previews* picture of Catwoman, it doesn't appear as if she's wearing a costume per se. What will her uniform consist of?
EB: She's wearing her full costume on the cover of the second issue, and that image was printed in the actual *Previews* article. She wears an Emma Peel style catsuit (which was my wife's idea) and a modified leather aviation helmet (or

whatever those things are called—Snoopy and Enemy Ace both wore them) with goggles that have infrared and other gadgets included.

ST: What gadgets, if any, will she be sporting? Anything like a cat-o-nine tails or cat-a-rangs or anything campy like that?
EB: She wears her whip as a belt, but she rarely uses it.

ST: Many people consider Bruce Wayne an unnecessary component to there actually "being" a Batman. Why does or doesn't Catwoman need Selina Kyle?
EB: There is no separation between the two. Catwoman is an extension of who Selina is, she's the voice of her conscience.

ST: How do you approach writing Catwoman as opposed to scribing the Dark Knight?
EB: I don't know. I just write them. With any character, you just learn who they are, and find what part you want to explore next about them.

ST: What are your goals with this series?
EB: To create an engaging comic with characters that readers will care about.

ST: Why did DC start the series over at issue one instead of continuing into the hundreds?
EB: After they saw the pencils for the first issue, and read it, they decided it was so different from what had come before that it was worth relaunching to try to attract new readers. I think it's a good idea, now that the book is coming out, finally; at the time, though, I wasn't all that thrilled. But comics fans are too obsessed with numbers anyway. I hope most will just be happy to have a good issue of *Catwoman* (assuming our comic is good).

ST: One of the best factors about her relationship with Batman was all the sexual tension between the two. How much of that will you explore in this series and what role will Batman have in this new series?
EB: Probably not as much as people would like. Honestly, it's been done to death, and it can never go anywhere, so what's the point. I want to do things in this book that aren't completely predictable from the outset, so an affair between Batman and Catwoman probably won't happen until I can get approval to really push the boundaries of what has come before. Otherwise it's just—she's hot for him, he'd like to do her, but it can never be.

After a hundred times, who cares anymore?

ST: What are Catwoman's strengths?
EB: Smaller breasts.

ST: What are her weaknesses?
EB: See above.

ST: [laughs] Ok, I can see where this conversation is heading, so let's switch gears. What version of Catwoman is your favorite?
EB: I don't know. I'm not really a big favorite-era guy, but if pushed, it would probably be the Earth 2 version where she married Bruce Wayne and the Huntress was their daughter.

ST: Ah, I like that version best, also. What about the TV or movie version of Catwoman?
EB: Julie Newmar, obviously.

ST: Who are some of the guest stars that Catwoman will encounter in this series?
EB: Slam Bradley, eventually, Wildcat . . . Crispus Allen from *Detective* and the upcoming *Gotham Central*. A few other surprises from the past, as well as mystery villains.

ST: Who's doing the art chores on this new Catwoman series?
EB: The first four issues, and the Slam Bradley lead-in in *Detective* are drawn by Darwyn Cooke, who is pretty much a comics genius. Mike Allred is also inking the first four issues. These comics are some of the most amazing things I have ever seen. Darwyn adds so much to what I write that it's insane. And he puts so much thought into how to use the space on each page. I was lucky to be able to work with him, because he's a good writer, too, and he has a lot of projects on his plate for the future, that he's writing himself, so I doubt many writers will have a chance to work with him. I can't say enough good things about what he's done.

After that, Brad Rader and Cameron Stewart are taking over as the regular team. Brad is another guy who came from the Bruce Timm storyboard studio and he's another guy who likes to really use the space on the page. Brad is doing amazing work as well, and just gets better every issue. He's really focused on the storytelling aspects of the comic, and he also will draw anything I ask him to, in an almost Dave Gibbons–like way. He's continuing the angle that Darwyn started, the dynamic action and the straightforward storytelling, though their styles are a little different, obviously.

ST: What do you do to overcome creative blocks when you're working?

EB: Answer interviews for *Sequential Tart*.

ST: What's the craziest thing that ever happened to you at a comic book convention?

EB: Once I puked off of Dave Sim's balcony at a party—this was in 1986, I think. Does that qualify? Nothing really crazy has ever happened *to* me, though, it's usually that I have done crazy things to other people. But that's all in the past. Ah, the '80s . . . What a different world it was. And we thought things seemed scary *then*.

ST: What other projects are you working on?

EB: So many, it seems. Currently, it's *Batman, Catwoman, Point Blank* for Wildstorm's mature line, then followed by *Sleeper* for the same line. I also will be co-writing *Gotham Central* with Greg Rucka, trading off every three issues or so. And there are some other projects in development, but not approved yet. I'm pretty much busy with just the stuff I have right now until about the end of 2002 at least.

Ed Brubaker Interview

KEITH GILES / 2001

Originally published in *Comic Book Resources*. 17 December 2001. Web. Reprinted by permission.

Ed Brubaker has got the tiger by the tail these days. He's gone from writing alternative comics to writing DC's flagship *Batman* comic and now he's on board as the writer for DC's *Catwoman* each month. Still, he finds time to launch a new book next year on Wildstorm's Mature line of comics starting with a five-issue miniseries called *Point Blank* and a spin-off ongoing series after that called *Sleepers*.

Brubaker talked with CBR about his upcoming work and gave a little insight into what makes his Batman different from the rest.

Keith Giles: Tell me about *Catwoman*. What new perspective do you bring?
Ed Brubaker: I guess it's different because I never read what came before (laughs). No, but really, I read what was pointed out to me by the editor as the more formative stuff, then I read from the beginning of Devin Grayson's run on. I don't know how different [my Catwoman] actually is from what came before, other than that what came before isn't necessarily the kind of thing I would write. The main thing that's different to me is that I'm trying to get into her as a character who obviously has a lot of internal conflict in her life and explore her character. I felt she lent herself to that film-noir kind of world, and luckily we were able to get [artist] Darwyn Cooke to draw it and he's totally comfortable in that kind of a world.

KG: How did the Slam Bradley series in *Detective* come about as the lead-in to the new *Catwoman* series?
EB: At first, when the editors were asking us to do this lead-in teaser-type thing—the back-ups in *Detective*—their suggestion was to do just a Selina

Kyle story where she wasn't Catwoman and show what she was doing before our first issue and I thought, you know, that it's more important to leave it vague what she was doing. So, I thought, let's have someone exploring her character and this will be a chance to point out everything I think is cool and important about her character. So, it turns out that Darwyn and I both really liked Slam Bradley as a character and wanted to use him.

For me, *Catwoman*, as a comic, has been too concerned about showing her always having to steal something. Like, every few issues some priceless diamond shipment is coming to Gotham and she's gotta go steal it. But you know, after a while, no one's going to bring their diamond shipments to Gotham.

KG: Yeah, you'd think . . . and if they did wouldn't they bring a small army along with them to guard it?

EB: Yeah, the Crown Jewels are not going to be on display! Plus, if you've been a professional thief for ten years, and you're as good as Catwoman is supposed to be, I mean, real professional thieves pull off like two, three jobs a year. And they're not kleptomaniacs. They're not doing it all the time and they don't get lured into stuff that they just can't pass up stealing. Those are the people who end up in jail.

KG: Right!

EB: If you were really some hot-shot thief, not only would she not steal that often, when she did she'd steal big. I also figure she's got millions stashed away in safety deposit boxes all over the country and in Gotham. So, I just thought, who is she? Where did she come from? The way you tell almost any story is to find out who the character is, what their background is, what's important to them, and try to discover which stories make sense for that character. The interesting thing to me is, looking at Selina Kyle, she's someone who was orphaned as a kid, raised in the system in the some of the worst conditions, ended up on the streets. But she's got to have some capacity for caring. I think she's only shown that, so far, with Batman really. Or in *Batman: Year One*, she showed some compassion for Holly, but that was it. So, why doesn't she care about other people like her? People who the system doesn't care about, the cops don't care about and who, really, Batman doesn't care about? That's kind of where I found a place to get Selina's stories from.

KG: Very interesting. No one's really thought about that side of things before.

EB: Well, I don't know if anyone else has ever thought of it before, they may have, (laughs) but that's what I'm doing.

KG: But most writers have approached Catwoman from the stereotypical cat-burglar character, who is very shallow as a person.

EB: I have the benefit of coming from outside mainstream comics. I spent my early twenties to my early thirties totally outside that world, doing alternative comics. Now I've come into this as sort of a crash course. When I first got offered the *Catwoman* book, I had just finished reading a series of Lawrence Block's *Matthew Scudder* books, he's a private detective. So, in these books, about halfway through, he just starts taking jobs for people who the cops wouldn't help. One of the books is about these criminals who were targeting drug dealers because they know they won't go to the cops and they're kidnapping their wives and saying, "Give us a million dollars or we'll send your wife back in pieces" and so they give them the million dollars and they get their wife back in pieces anyway. The cops wouldn't really help them. The cops would just be like, "So, where'd you get the million dollars?" So, this was a brilliant crime. I looked at that and I thought, "That's the way to approach Catwoman." Like Matt Scudder, he's a PI whose best friend is a criminal and that's a lot like Selina Kyle, who is a criminal and who happens to be a pretty cool person underneath it all.

KG: So, what surprises do you have in store for us with *Catwoman*?

EB: Uhmm . . . sheesh. I guess I could, but I feel like the way comics are now so much is spoiled ahead of time. It's not like reading *TV Guide* to see what next week's show's about, I mean, people are reading *Previews* now. You gotta figure like maybe 20 percent of people who are buying comics now read *Previews*, maybe more. So, everyone's months ahead. I'm like ten months ahead on *Catwoman* and you've got to reach a point where you either care or don't care about stories being spoiled.

KG: Well, you don't have to spoil anything for us.

EB: Ok, I won't.

KG: So, will we see any of the other Bat-family members show up in *Catwoman*?

EB: Batman, yes. A couple of other characters from Gotham City are in there, but I'm trying to stick as far away from any crossovers or continuity tangles as possible. Like, with *Catwoman* we never mention the whole "Bruce Wayne Murderer" storylines coming up. One of the cops from *Detective Comics* shows up and there will be a few other characters in there. Who knows, Wildcat might even show up someday. It's kind of like a big noir soap opera. I kind of started out thinking I'd just do a year on the book and then I wrote up until

Fig. 4: A less glamorous Catwoman in a pulp fiction crime world (complete with pulp-era detective Slam Bradley) in *Catwoman* Vol. 3, #7. (From *Catwoman* Vol. 3 #7 by Ed Brubaker and Brad Rader © DC Comics; originally published by DC Comics in 2002; available in *Catwoman: Crooked Little Town*)

issue six and I thought this is some of the best writing I've done. It's really cool to be writing a superhero comic that isn't Batman. I mean, Batman is the coolest job in the world, but there's all this continuity with him. Batman's like the most popular comic book character of the twentieth century. There's not a lot I do that gets sent back to me from the editors, but I know that I can't shake things up too much. There are major meetings about changes to Batman's world. Everybody has to sign off on any major stuff. But, with *Catwoman* it's just me and my editor and whatever we want to do with *Catwoman*, that's it. Catwoman's a major DC character and everyone wants to use her in their book. Darwyn and I have basically redesigned her look and now if she appears in *The Flash* or something, she's going to look the way we designed her. Not with a tail or the purple costume. There's times I wish I could do what James Robinson did with *Starman* and do the book for six or seven years and then kill the character off at the end. (Laughs)

KG: She's mine and no one else can use her. (Laughs)

EB: But I'm really into most everything I'm writing now.

KG: So, what was the first indie comic you did?

EB: I did a comic in 1989 for Slave Labor called *Purgatory USA* sort of a precursor to *Lowlife*. The stuff in *Lowlife* kind of came out of those.

KG: Autobiographical stories?

EB: It's nothing I want people to seek out, really.

KG: How did you get that gig?

EB: I started off as a cartoonist. I always wanted to do my own stuff. When I was a kid, I wanted to be a penciller and I really wanted to draw Spider-Man or Captain America, and then I discovered *Cerebus* and *Love and Rockets* as I got older and got turned on to this whole other world. I always felt like my art wasn't "Superhero-y" enough. But, then I thought, if Dave Sim can do it, I can do it. But, then as you grow up as a cartoonist, hopefully, you actually start to get an appreciation for the history of the comics medium. Instead of just looking at Hanna-Barbera and saying those guys can't draw. I mean, wait a second! (Laughs)

I spent so many years doing indie stuff that now I'm amazed at people's opinions of art and comics. Everyone's got this bizarre idea of what's good art and what isn't.

I remember being at a convention as a teenager seeing Scott Shaw! These kids came up and were looking at some art he'd done for some Cocoa Pebbles stuff and one of the kids said, "Do you ever wish that you could draw good so you could draw Spider-Man or Superman?" and he said, "Well, I think I do draw good. This is how I wanted to draw my whole life!" I mean, arguably his was a much more commercial style than the guy who was drawing *X-Men* at the time and they're looking at a page that, in the early eighties, he was paid like five thousand dollars for. That kind of opened my eyes and then I got into the alternative comics where everyone has their own style and started learning about cartooning as an art form. Then I realized that this tiny genre of superheroes owes a lot to those people in the early days that a lot people who read comics don't even know about.

KG: Very true. Especially in America it's all about the icons and superheroes.
EB: And one of my favorite current cartoonists is Don Rosa and I haven't been able to read his stuff for like five years now because he does stuff only in Europe. Nobody publishes his Uncle Scrooge comics in America and that's just ridiculous.

KG: Yes it is. So, to change gears here, what do you think about how your *Deadenders* comic fared?
EB: I actually thought *Deadenders* would be an amazingly huge commercial comic! (Laughs) Vertigo needed a teen comic and I thought that WB would probably make a TV show out of it and it had scooters in it and kids who are into scooters will buy anything with scooters in it. Actually, I think, now that it's all over, I think it would make a more successful television show. Everytime WB is looking for new material I hope that *Deadenders* will get noticed.

KG: Well, what if the series had continued? Were there plots you didn't get to develop?
EB: I had planned through issue twenty-four and it got to the point where it wasn't going that good and then I wanted to end it at issue eighteen and then suddenly my six-issue plan got cut into a three-issue plan.

KG: So, you did plan an ending?
EB: Well, I did plan to do it for two years. There were things I could've done after that, but if the book had been more popular I could've written stories about the other kids in the book.

KG: Do you have a preference as a writer for more realistic stories as opposed to the superhero stories?

EB: I don't know, probably. I feel a little hemmed in by *Batman*, sometimes, because it's *Batman*. Every single issue has to be about Batman and there's a certain amount of action I've got to have in every single issue but you know I just look at that as my constraint and do my best. Sometimes I've succeeded, sometimes I've failed.

KG: You're big on characters, are there things left to tell about Batman? How many hundreds of stories have been written about this guy?

EB: The idea is to find new things. I'm pretty sure I'm the first guy who's ever shown Bruce Wayne's first kiss. There may have been something in the fifties. But I just try to look at the comics that have gone before and I say, "For me, this is the way to take this character," and the problem is that there's so many people working on Batman every month. Three books a month have Batman as the main character and then there's every member of the supporting cast with their own books where he appears as a supporting cast member and then Batman is in the JLA and half the time he's in Superman or some other comics too.

   I hate to sound like I'm grousing about Batman. But it's the one book that I work on where I have to worry about that stuff and crossovers. Especially when we're in the middle of a big storyline where everyone takes part in a bigger story. Usually we just get a big bag every month with xeroxes of every-one's issues after they've been inked and lettered, but now we're at the stage where we're reading each other's scripts to make sure we don't overlap.

KG: Like if someone gives him a scar over his eye . . .

EB: Yeah, make sure you don't put it over the wrong eye in your book. Right. There was actually, in January, a place where Devin and I wrote the exact same scene and she chose to take this one spin on hers and so I had to rewrite like half of the dialog in my scene since mine shipped after hers.

   I'm clean-up every month since Batman ships last.

KG: How would you define the Brubaker *Batman*? When people are looking back at your tenure on this book, how do you want them to remember your work?

EB: Well, the best *Batman* ever! (Laughs) I'm sadly not much of a Batman historian, but I felt like the Batman of the fifties, sixties, and early seventies that was the coolest stuff. The comics in the nineties looked like it was too tied up together, not too easy to jump in. I think they're pretty accessible now though.

KG: Is there anything that sets your *Batman* title apart from the other titles out there now?

EB: I think I explore the Bruce Wayne side more than the other books out there. Devin Grayson did focus a little on (Bruce) with all that psychoanalysis stuff that was written by Bruce Wayne about his friends. But she's interested in how Batman relates to the rest of the Bat-family as the really screwed-up patriarch of the family. Whereas I'm more interested in exploring more of the tragedy angle where Bruce is more of the fractured persona and the Bruce Wayne part of him never really lived beyond the age he was when his parents got killed. After that he was really Batman only pretending to be Bruce Wayne sometimes. I thought that was fascinating, and I thought that was really screwed up.

KG: Oh yeah.

EB: Well, there are stories there, obviously. I've really tried to bring more humanistic stuff to it, more emotional impact to the stories. Not to suggest that they haven't always had it, but that's what I'm more interested in, more of the human element.

KG: So, tell me about your Wildstorm Mature stuff that's coming out.

EB: So far I'm working on one book for them. I start in January on the other book. One is called *Sleeper* and that is a spin-off of the miniseries that Colin Wilson is drawing called *Point Blank*. It's kind of a weird project that sort of randomly happened where I had been talking about doing some creator-owned work through Homage and Scott Dunbier had an idea about a murder mystery comic in the Wildstorm Universe. Then it ended up being part of the Wildstorm Mature line and so Scott asked if I had any ideas as an ongoing and at first I thought about it and I said I was doing too much superhero stuff at the moment. Then I thought about it for like five minutes more and I called him back up and said, "Ok, I've got a great idea!" So, that's *Sleeper*. I basically pitched it as "Donnie Brasco as a superhero" because he's a superhero who is pretending to be a supervillain.

KG: Very cool.

EB: Well, it's kind of a very obvious idea. (Laughs) But I told Scott that I'm tired of worrying about preventing a crime. The villain has more of a complex character at times than the hero. Of course, no supervillain has been able to carry their own comic. Not even Doctor Doom or the Joker, who are like the two most popular villains out there. So, I was thinking that the way to do it was like that Playstation video game *Driver*. Have you played that?

KG: Oh yeah, I've got that one.

EB: I remember thinking at the time how funny it was that you couldn't just be a criminal in that game. You had to be a cop pretending to be a criminal.

KG: Which, of course, justifies everyone you crash into and everything you destroy.

EB: Right. So, then I realized I had to change the miniseries around to make it work. It started out that, in *Point Blank*, somebody gets murdered and Grifter is like really pissed and throwing people through windows and blowing people's heads off and trying to kill the guys who killed his friend. I describe it as "*Get Carter* meets *The Watchmen*," sort of a deconstructionist superhero story about a guy on the rampage. He's on a slow rampage, 'cause he's trying to solve this mystery but he's just a guy, he's not like Batman or Sherlock Holmes. So, then I had to change it so there wasn't a murder. Now, the person who was supposed to get killed is actually alive on life support. So, (in *Sleeper*) the main character is a good guy pretending to be a bad guy but the only one who knows the truth is on life support.

Plus, a lot of what inspired me was stuff like the John Le Carré novels where he talks about the way people get made into double-agents where they have no choice and there's some of that in there. The title *Sleeper* comes from the espionage term for a double-agent. I got that from Greg Rucka actually. I couldn't come up with a name for the book and I talked to him and he immediately suggested *Sleeper* and I went public with the name as soon as I could so no one else could produce another book next year with the same title.

KG: Which Wildstorm characters will we be seeing?

EB: Well, in *Point Blank*, Grifter of course, some of the Authority, characters from Wildcats, Team7, and Gen 13—but not in costume—because one of the things about having these guys in your mature readers book is not to mention their superhero names and not have them in costume.

KG: Of course. So, when are these coming out?

EB: I think in May, *Point Blank* starts, and *Sleeper* follows that directly. Sean Phillips will be doing the *Sleeper* artwork for us.

An ORCA Q&A with Ed Brubaker

TIM O'SHEA / 2003

Originally published in *Comic Book Electronic Magazine* 422 (30 May 2003). Web. Reprinted by permission.

Ed Brubaker has helped reinvigorated the Batman universe, simply put. And now he's dabbling with the Wildstorm universe through the new series, *Sleeper*. Fortunately, in between writing various titles, this master of comics noir granted me an e-interview. I wish to thank Ed for his time and thoughts. Enjoy.

O'Shea: *Sleeper* is a very ambitious work, with a great deal going on already in just four issues out. How do you strike a balance between giving the reader a great deal of content and not oversaturating the book with varying elements to the point of distraction?

Brubaker: It's always a struggle with *Sleeper*, really. I wish I had thirty or forty pages an issue to tell the story each month, but I don't, so I try to experiment with the storytelling, using a lot of cutaway scenes and layering in flashbacks to make the story more dense and at the same time keep it moving forward. After the first issue, which I rewrote six times, it's become kind of instinctual.

O'Shea: Correct me if I'm wrong, while I know that some of your work is influenced by film noir (and the work of your uncle, John Paxton), but also I sensed a bit of Steranko's *S.H.I.E.L.D.* Did you read that run and would you say it influenced you at all as a writer? (And if I am wrong, in addition to film noir, what comic creators influence your approach toward writing?)

Brubaker: Actually, while I always enjoyed the ideas and the presentation of the artwork, I'm not really a huge fan of Steranko's work. I liked his art a lot as a kid, but by the time I discovered *S.H.I.E.L.D.*, I was too old to appreciate it, I

Fig. 5: Holden Carver, after infiltrating a super-criminal organization, finds himself in yet another impossible moral situation in *Sleeper* Vol. 2, #7. (From *Sleeper* Vol. 2, #7 by Ed Brubaker and Sean Phillips © DC Comics; originally published by Wildstorm in 2005; available in *Sleeper: All False Moves*)

think. Like a lot of the mainstream work of the '60s and '70s, the actual writing is nothing to write home about. There's just a ton of overwriting in comics from that time period, useless captions and a lot of expository dialog.

As for noir films, I do love a lot of them, and my favorite old film is probably *Out of the Past*. I don't know how much any specific film influenced my work, though; it's more just the themes and the tone of noir that seeps into some of my stuff. It's all very character-driven stuff, and that's what I do, really. Noir extends beyond film, too, and I would say it's writers like James M. Cain and Jim Thompson and Fredric Brown and a few others who really had an influence on me. And of course, on the other side of noir you've got the private eye drama and Ross Macdonald, whose work holds so much sway over me most of the time that I feel almost beholden to it. He took what Chandler and Hammett did right, and added a level of mythology and personal tragedy and, I think, wrote the best mysteries of the twentieth century.

Comic writers, I don't know, developmentally, I think Alan Moore probably had the biggest overall influence, because he did so many different kinds of story well, and made me think about things differently. I'd also list Harvey Pekar and Gilbert Hernandez as pretty big influences, especially when I discovered their work in the early '80s.

O'Shea: According to your website, elements of *Gotham Noir* are based on "real-life mysteries from the history of Manhattan." Can you point to any real-life events that help shape your plotting or approaches on the current series you write?

Brubaker: Oh, there are always some real life events that spark story ideas. I once said that when you start writing mysteries almost everything you hear about sounds like an idea you could spin a story around. What are some recent ones? In *Catwoman* #5 there was a story about kids being mules for drug smuggling, and while I was taking something I'd read about (immigrants being forced to mule drugs) and changing it around, a week after the comic came out a big story broke about a guy running a ring of child mules. In general, especially on a book like *Gotham Central*, I just try to make the crimes seem like something from real life. The three events from *Gotham Noir* were interesting stories that I thought could tie together well—the disappearance of Judge Crater (Judge Pitt in the comic), the investigation into bribery at the mayor's office in the '30s and '40s, and a drowning death of a wealthy girl who turned out to have been molested as a child by a prominent politician. I took all those and added them into the tale of Gordon as a washed-up drunk and a shell-shocked WW2 veteran.

O'Shea: Also at your website, in discussing Batman, you mention a hope that you are "bringing some humanism to the work" I think you are, but I wonder, do you feel (as some writers do) that Bruce Wayne is a mask for Batman, and if not, what is your perspective on Wayne?

Brubaker: That was what the previous editorial regime did to the character, really, and I never really agreed with it. Maybe it works to some degree, for specific stories, but in the end, it makes Bruce Wayne the least evolved character in his own comics, and it's really kind of a stupid distinction to make unless you're trying to say he's a split personality. Why should Bruce Wayne be any different than, say, Wally West (the Flash)? They're both the civilian identity of a costumed hero. I don't see why there was ever this obsession with dividing Batman like that except to make him seem more driven and robotic, and that's frankly, not a good way to use Batman, because it makes it impossible to have him connect with anyone on an emotional level. That's why we did that whole "Bruce Wayne: Fugitive" storyline, to be able to get back to the human side of him.

O'Shea: I was pleasantly surprised to see you express a fondness for the late Dick Sprang's work on Batman, what is it about his approach that you appreciated and how (if it all) does it influence your approach toward the character?

Brubaker: I just read a lot of Finger/Sprang stories in *Batman* from the '30s to the '70s as a kid and loved them. I reread the whole book recently and still enjoyed them a lot. I think I like the innocence and invention that were in the comics then, and they had drama, too, it was just more like *Dick Tracy* or something. As far as how those stories influenced me, I have basically done "Ultimate" versions of two of them—the Lew Moxon story where Bruce Wayne's father has a run-in with the mob at a costume party, and the second Two Face story, which I took inspiration from to create the new Bat-villain, the Charlatan in my first story in *Detective Comics*. The character of Paul Sloan goes back to the '50s, and I just changed his origin to make him more twisted and scary.

O'Shea: Given the number of Bat titles and his status of one of the three DC icons, how hard is it to tell a unique story with the character? Do you worry about that or do you just focus on telling a good story?

Brubaker: It's a bit of both, really; you worry and then you just try to shove it all aside and focus on your own story while you can. I mean, with Batman, there's so much material constantly flowing out there, in the monthlies, and so much backstory, you can get lost if you let yourself, and that'll stop you from writing anything decent at all.

O'Shea: In essence, starting from scratch (pardon the pun) with the new *Catwoman* series, were there any runs or writers (not necessarily even connected to Catwoman) that inspired your take on the character?

Brubaker: The biggest influences on Catwoman are probably Frank Miller's *Daredevil* and Lawrence Block's Matt Scudder books. Not that the book really feels like either of those, but I think Miller's DD was probably the best example of what I was hoping to do on a monthly non-powered hero book. He really delved into the characters and created a cast to explore outside the main hero, which is all things I've been doing in *Catwoman*.

O'Shea: If given the chance would you do a Slam Bradley mini- or maxiseries?

Brubaker: In a heartbeat. There almost was one, but it got stalled and then it didn't happen, but maybe someday. It has to be drawn by Javier Pulido, though.

O'Shea: Do you feel you've succeeded (both by your own standards and with the audience) in accomplishing what you set out to do with *Catwoman*, so far?

Brubaker: That's not really for me to say, but I hope so. I think the book is as close to how I envisioned it at the start, before anything was on paper and I just had some ideas, as it could be. I think it's nice, too, that on the whole it's one of the DCU's best reviewed books.

O'Shea: How hard is it, as a writer, to try to establish a relationship with the new commissioner (Michael Akins) and Batman, when you have the fan favorite James Gordon back in the narrative landscape to use again?

Brubaker: I'm not worried about it, honestly. Some people complain that we haven't learned enough about Akins yet, and I just say, give it time. He's only been around a few years. Gordon was around for about thirty before he had a personality, even.

O'Shea: In writing *Gotham Central*, do you make a concerted effort to avoid using the "capes" or are the capes part of the equation always, even in this book?

Brubaker: We just do whatever feels natural for each story. We've got no mandate to use or not use the capes. But it is *GOTHAM Central*, and it's

Fig. 6: Marcus Driver, a frustrated police detective, takes out his anger on Batman, one of the few successful crime-fighters in Gotham City in *Gotham Central* Vol. 1, #2. (From *Gotham Central* Vol. 1, #2 by Ed Brubaker, Greg Rucka, and Michael Lark © DC Comics; originally published by DC Comics in 2003; available in *Gotham Central: In the Line of Duty*)

supposed to be about being a cop in THAT city, the city with Batman, and Arkham Asylum, and the Joker. So it makes sense that we'd see them from time to time, otherwise it would just be *HOMICIDE*.

O'Shea: I really enjoyed *Scene of the Crime* and wondered, would you and Mr. Lark ever consider revisiting the character of Jack Herriman?
Brubaker: We always talk about it, but it's a problem of scheduling, really. Also, we're hoping if we do another *Scene of the Crime*, to do it as an original GN, not a miniseries, so we need to wait until we have the clout to do it that way. Which may be never, but I'm keeping my hopes up.

Interview with Ed Brubaker

KULJIT MITHRA / 2006

Originally published in *Daredevil: ManWithoutFear.Com*. June 2006. Web. Reprinted by permission.

With the fifth issue of "The Devil in Cell-Block D" out this week, writer Ed Brubaker chats with me about what's come before and what is ahead for Daredevil.

Many thanks to Ed Brubaker for taking time out of his busy schedule to do the interview!

There is discussion about the current arc and Civil War, so please be warned about possible spoilers!

Kuljit Mithra: When Brian Bendis and Alex Maleev announced they were leaving *Daredevil*, yours and Michael Lark's names instantly came up as the next creative team in rumors online . . . it seemed like a logical choice then and after four issues into "Devil in Cell-Block D," you've made a seamless transition from their run. I've read that Bendis worked with you before he left and he only decided to have Matt in prison in his final issue after you wanted to work with this predicament. How much of that is true, and what was the appeal for you as a writer to take Matt through this kind of story?

Ed Brubaker: What happened was, Brian told me he was leaving DD, and for a few weeks, I thought, do I want to write that book? Especially following such an amazing run? And so I kicked some ideas around, thinking, what could you do, to follow that, what would the next logical step be? And I decided, you could either undo the Identity problem and revert to the old status quo, or you could take what Brian did and run with it as far as you can—and to me, that meant putting Matt behind bars. I called up Bendis and asked him what he thought, and he said something like—I've been wanting to end my run with him in jail, but I figured that'd be too mean to whoever followed, but if that's where you want to take him, then why not start with him there? So, really, the only thing that changed for me was how quickly he got to prison. He was going to be put there at the end of my first arc, initially, but this was even better. I got to jump right into the deep end, and I loved that we actually had a hand-off with a cliff-hanger ending, in some ways. That's never done in comics these days.

Mithra: How did Bendis plan to leave DD if he couldn't end it with Matt in prison?

Brubaker: I don't know. We never got that far. I suspect, with four wives in Utah.

Mithra: Was there ever a point in time when you weren't going to be the next writer? Did you have to write a proposal? And has it now differed in execution?

Brubaker: I think it was one of those everyone knew but me kind of things. Brian was saying it was a done deal long before I ever got the call from Joe Q that it was mine. I did write an outline of the first year or so, but that was after I had the gig. Most of what I did was talk to Joe Q about what I'd like to do, and what his thoughts were. He's very careful with DD.

Mithra: What do you believe worked and didn't work in the Bendis/Maleev run? For the most part, I saw a division . . . many hated it, many loved it. There didn't seem to be an in-between.

Brubaker: My only complaint is a really minor one. I think Alex's fight scenes were a little stiff in some places. I think his art in general, and the mood and tone he set for the book are amazing, though, and he's one of my favorite artists. Other than that, I think they did a hell of a job. Maybe the best extended run on any character in Marvel history. I liked that they took risks—whole issues without Matt in costume, the Decalogue arc, hell man, those guys had balls the size of the S.H.I.E.L.D. helicarrier. It's because of how good they were that Michael and I keep trying our hardest on our run, I think.

Mithra: What's your opinion on spoilers now being released as part of the solicitations? Your first issue was basically spoiled by the preview cover art for DD82.

Brubaker: It's a mixed bag, honestly. If you play things too closely to the vest, keep too much secret until publishing, then orders stay stagnant. If you reveal too much, though, online fans get spoiled. I wish there was a way to

Fig. 7: Matt Murdock/Daredevil makes a deal with the Kingpin, another moral compromise informed by the relative moral framework of prison life in *Daredevil* Vol. 2, #84. (From *Daredevil* Vol. 2, #84 by Ed Brubaker and Michael Lark © Marvel; originally published by Marvel in 2006; available in *Daredevil: Inside and Out, Vol. 1*)

just show retailers the upcoming stuff, but it doesn't work, it always leaks out. For DD82, though, revealing Matt in prison, Marvel got Brian's permission before they released that, because it was more about the end of his run, than mine. The issue with Foggy's grave on the cover, though, I'm okay with that going out, because our sales went up a lot on our second issue, and according to Marvel, they keep going up since then, so obviously, it's a very mixed bag. People want to be spoiled, so they know what to buy, but then they don't, too.

Mithra: Judging from your knowledge of DD continuity, is it safe to say you've been a fan of DD for a long time, or has your DD reading been the "major" arcs, like the Miller stories, "Born Again," etc.? Any favorite creators? Any DD arcs that you aren't a fan of?

Brubaker: I'm a longtime DD fan, but I confess, my knowledge is more sporadic than I wish it was. I've read runs of the book over the years in the '70s and '80s, but I quit regularly reading it not long after "Born Again," probably, until the MK editions started. Since then, I've read what I can find of the stuff in between, and reread the earlier stuff that's available, but unlike Cap, DD issues aren't so easy to find, or affordable. When I got the Cap gig, within three months, I was able to buy almost every issue in one form or another for a few hundred dollars, maybe, thanks to ebay. With DD, there are not so many runs of fifty issues for sale online.

My favorite DD creators would be Gene Colan, Frank Miller, Klaus Janson, David Mazzuchelli, Bendis and Maleev, and Quesada, whose "DD: Father" I'm really enjoying . . . And I know how it ends, too.

Arcs I'm not a fan of? That's a loaded question, isn't it? I guess, of the stuff I heard was great that I searched out, I was a bit surprised by the few Chichester and Nocenti issues I could track down. They just didn't do much for me. Great art, interesting stories, but something just didn't click for me. Maybe I read the wrong issues.

Mithra: Since you've written Batman, and many fans compare DD to Batman often, do you think it's fair to make this comparison? Are they really that similar to you? What do you believe is their greatest difference?

Brubaker: Well, the greatest difference would be that DD actually has powers, sort of. His radar sense, his hearing, smell, etc., make him a much different character to handle than Batman. I was just dealing with this, having a character lie to Matt, and realizing he should know, and trying to think of why he doesn't. Other than that, though, I see them as vastly different. Matt is working class, and Bruce is from old money and privilege. Matt isn't as angry as Bruce most of the time. Otherwise, they're both guys is tights who like statues and the rain, a lot.

Oh, and the public doesn't know Bruce Wayne is Batman.

Mithra: As part of this first arc, you've had Foggy (seemingly) killed, brought back some old DD supporting cast, and brought in others . . . I'm going to throw out some character's names . . . can you describe how you view them and if applicable, why you chose to use them, and if at all possible, hint at what you have in store for them?

Let's start with Foggy Nelson.

Brubaker: My favorite character in the book, in some ways. It hurt to shank him, but he gets another hurrah in a few issues, so at least I got to write him some more. His death was very important to our story, though, for what it did to Matt.

Mithra: Ben Urich.

Brubaker: You can't write DD without using Urich, it's like a law, I think. He's a great guy, because he's so real and human. He doesn't always do the right thing, because he's scared, and yet, at the end of the day, he's one of Matt's best friends. It was a lot of fun writing that issue from Ben's POV and playing with the old "My name is Ben Urich, I'm a reporter" thing, too.

Mithra: Dakota North.

Brubaker: I obviously couldn't use Jessica Jones, so I dragged out Dakota North from obscurity, because I was a fan of her old miniseries that Tony Salmons drew. Only to find out that C. B. Cebulski already had a new mini pitch for her in at Marvel.

Mithra: Becky Blake.

Brubaker: One of my favorites from the Miller-era cast, and I couldn't figure out why she wasn't in the book, so I brought her back. I like her attitude, so I gave her a law degree, to help with Matt's case.

Mithra: Morgan.

Brubaker: As an old-school Cap fan, I always liked Morgan. He was basically the black kingpin of Harlem. When looking for gangleaders for the Ryker's arc, I knew I'd need racial division, sadly, because that's how prison life is, segregated, so I grabbed him from the ether as well. His duel canes are a reference to him being crippled in an issue of *Black Panther*, I think, as well as a nod to Orson Welles' *The Lady from Shanghai*, which has a dogged reporter hobbling about on two canes—an image that stuck with me for twenty years, since I first saw that movie. A masterpiece of noir, for those who haven't seen it.

Mithra: Hammerhead.
Brubaker: Just always liked him, and he's white. He's a dumb character, but I like his flat head.

Mithra: Black Tarantula.
Brubaker: A character I discovered only because I couldn't use the Tarantula, because he's dead. However, LaMuerto really grew on me, so look for him to return to the pages of DD in the future, in a big way.

Mithra: Bullseye.
Brubaker: What needs to be said?

Mithra: Kingpin.
Brubaker: Again. He's a lynchpin to the first year of our run, so I couldn't do it without him.

Mithra: Punisher.
Brubaker: I'd have included him just to get his opening scene in, because it's so funny. His role in the first arc was very important, though, to show Matt a counterpoint to where he was heading.

Mithra: Alton Lennox.
Brubaker: Mystery man. You'll meet him in the next arc, though who he is, and what he's doing are mysteries.

Mithra: The other Daredevil.
Brubaker: One of my all-time favorite Marvel characters. Nuff said.

Mithra: Any DD characters that you will never use?
Brubaker: Not off the top of my head.

Mithra: I believe you've mentioned that the other Daredevil's identity will be revealed at the end of this arc . . . so will it be "resolved" in the title, or in *Civil*

Fig. 8: Peace and prayer found by Matt Murdock/Daredevil only in the deepest of depths in *Daredevil* Vol. 1, #500. (From *Daredevil* Vol. 1, #500 by Ed Brubaker and Michael Lark © Marvel; originally published by Marvel in 2009; available in *Daredevil: The Return of the King*)

War? And how closely will the title tie-in with the events in *Civil War*, since we've seen "Daredevil" in issue 1?

Brubaker: DD doesn't really tie-in to *Civil War* at all. The other DD is in it, but his identity is revealed to readers in issue 87. Who he is, and what he's doing in CW, though, are like Easter Eggs for the DD readers following that book. They've got a really cool idea planned that I don't want to spoil.

Mithra: You've collaborated with Michael Lark on a variety of projects . . . why do you think it works? Is it a constant back and forth of ideas? Do you write your stories geared towards how he will draw it? Reason I ask is that some writers I've interviewed have said they've never even spoken with the people they've worked with.

Brubaker: Michael and I are like brothers. We love each other, but we bicker about the stories and art all the time. I think that's why it works, maybe, because we demand a lot from each other. Sometimes having Michael on a book is like having an extra editor, because he'll point out some story flaw I didn't even notice and I'll have to rewrite the ending or something. As far as working for him, I never even think about it now, it's just a natural process after eight years or so.

Mithra: And the final question, obviously you can't reveal the ending of this arc, but can you hint at what's ahead? How far into the future have you plotted and now with your current workload, how long do you plan on sticking with this title?

Brubaker: I'd like to stay one issue longer than Brian. Ha. As for what's ahead, hopefully stuff readers will like it as much as the tension of the prison drama. There'll be some globetrotting, some swashbuckling (a little, at least), a lot of noir tension and action, and the return of two villains that haven't been seen for a while (one who's always been totally ridiculous). And, we'll finally find out who's been manipulating Matt's life since he got tossed in Rykers, and the answer will shock you.

Oh yeah, and Mike Murdock . . . I'm not joking.

The Right to Remain Violent: Brubaker Talks "Criminal"

DAVE RICHARDS / 2006

Originally published in *Comic Book Resources*. 3 October 2006. Web. Reprinted by permission.

Ed Brubaker and Sean Phillips are hoping crime does pay because their new creator-owned series *Criminal* from Marvel's Icon imprint hits stores this Wednesday. The new ongoing series follows a large cast of interconnected characters and the various felonious acts they often engage in. CBR News spoke with writer Ed Brubaker about the crime series

Criminal came about when Brubaker and Phillips, who had previously collaborated on the Wildstorm series *Sleeper*, were searching for another project to work on. "I wanted it to be a truly creator-owned comic and hopefully something that like *Sleeper* would spawn a franchise of trade paperbacks," Brubaker told CBR News. "I started looking through some of my notebooks and I found all these outlines for crime stories I'd written. There was a time about four years ago when I was trying to sell a series of graphic novels to a foreign publisher. I had a bunch of notes from that and I looked at those and thought, 'Is there some way I can do a crime comic as a creator-owned thing that uses all these ideas and is like an umbrella title with a cast full of characters that I can populate these stories with and explore the themes that I have been fascinated with for years?'

"I sat down with that for a few days and was trying to figure out a way that would work as a continuing series as opposed to a series of graphic novels or miniseries," Brubaker continued. "So, I figured out this cast of characters who all have these links between them and the backstory of it all just started falling into place about a year or so ago. So it's been formulating in my head for all that time."

This large cast of characters Brubaker has developed for *Criminal* will populate their own little universe and some of them will take the stage and be the focus of the story at different times, similar to how certain characters receive the spotlight in titles like *Sin City* or *100 Bullets*. "One of my favorite crime writers is George Pelecanos," said Brubaker. "All his books take place in Washington DC. He's got a variety of different characters that sometimes star in a book. When you've got a book with one character, at some point in that story he hangs out with one of the characters from one of the other books. I always liked that. It was like all these characters exist in the George Pelecanos Universe. That was my break through as to, 'How do I make this my sort of Ed Brubaker universe?'

"There's a backstory to it all," Brubaker continued. "Basically all the characters interact, but the main character in the first arc is this guy Leo. There's a secret backstory that sort of gets pieced together through each arc, and when we get to the point where the reader thinks they know the entire backstory, then we're going to do sort of a period piece that's all about these characters when they were kids. That's when this backstory event happened."

The main characters in *Criminal* are acquainted with each other as adults because of their shared childhoods. "The main characters are all like second- or third-generation professional criminals," Brubaker said. "Their parents were all in a group that would pull down scores. So, their parents all knew each other and they have this twisted history of having grown up around each other. You know how your parents would sometimes take you to their work parties when you were a kid? Well, all their work parties ended with people getting in fist fights and broken glass. They weren't nice people."

Leo, the main character of the first arc of *Criminal*, tries to keep clear of violent displays of criminality like fist fights and broken glass. "He is a pickpocket and also has worked on a number of heists," Brubaker explained. "He is sort of one of those guys that if you're going to plan a score, you want to him to help you figure out how to get away with it, but being careful is really his big concern. His dad died in prison and he doesn't ever want to meet that same fate. He carries around a lot of guilt for some things and we don't exactly know why. He's a very careful, calculated person. He doesn't have a lot of friends and he doesn't let a lot of people in. He's one of those guys that any job he's ever worked, he always has another way out. He has multiple exits if he needs to take them and at the first sign that things are going wrong he will be the first person out the door, changing clothes, getting on a subway train and disappearing into the city.

"So, because of that he's got a little bit of a bad reputation among the criminal community," Brubaker continued. "A lot of people who don't really know him think that he's a coward. The people who have grown up with him, some of them don't really understand everything about him and think he's a coward as opposed to somebody who's just incredibly careful."

The first story arc finds a reluctant Leo joining a crew to take down a score. "It's a heist story," Brubaker stated. "A lot of them will be. I'm trying to do what will sort of be my ultimate noir because I want to start big. I decided to take a bunch of different noir genre tropes and string them into one story. The first act of the first story is basically a heist. The second act is sort of the twisted noir love story. The third act is sort of the 'man on the run gets revenge' noir story. They all string together into one sort of mini epic. It's the story of Leo taking a chance for a variety of reasons and how it completely backfires because he breaks his own rules. The one time he says 'fuck it' and puts his rules away, everything that could go wrong does. So, there was a reason for the rules."

As readers see the consequences of Leo breaking his own rules, they will also encounter a number of colorful and crooked characters. "Basically there's a crooked cop, and a guy from Leo's past named Seymour gets together with him to help plot this score," Brubaker said. "They have their own agenda obviously. Once Leo is convinced to go into it he brings in his friend Donnie who is this conman. He's an epileptic conman who makes a few thousand dollars a week pretending to have seizures on the train and asking people for money to go to the emergency room."

The character of Donnie was inspired by real events. "It's actually something I saw in real life in San Francisco," Brubaker explained. "There was a woman who I saw do this about six times. Then about a year later there was an article about her in the paper and how she was making like $4,000 a week. She had kids and lived in a penthouse apartment in San Francisco."

In addition to Donnie, Leo, Seymour, and the crooked cops, the heist crew also includes a female member. "Greta is sort of the other main character in the story," Brubaker stated. "She's this woman with a connection to Leo's past that sort of coerces him into helping out with this score because he feels somewhat responsible for something that happened to her in the past. They have sort of a cantankerous relationship because he doesn't really trust her for a variety of reasons but he feels beholden to her as well. They have a little bit of a struggle because even though they don't totally trust each other, they trust the other people on the job, a bunch of crooked cops and the people who hang out with them, even less. So it's an interesting dynamic; as they plot out the heist, everybody is wondering how they are going to get stabbed in the back or if they're going to walk away with millions of dollars."

This first story arc featuring Leo is called "Coward" and will run five parts. Leo will participate in the next story arc, but in a smaller capacity. "The next storyline is called 'Lawless' and that sort of ties into some of the stuff discussed in the backup stories in the first few issues," Brubaker said. "Each issue we're having various articles and backup stories and things like that because we have the full thirty-two pages to work with.

"The first backup story is about the wake of this guy who is mentioned in the first story arc," Brubaker continued. "In the backup story you find out that he's been dead for a while and the second storyline is about his older brother coming back to town because he just found out his brother was killed a year earlier. He comes back to town to find out what the hell is going on and he goes AWOL from the military, where he's been for about twenty years. He comes back looking for answers. It's kind of like *Get Carter* in a way. It's sort of the investigative noir trope."

The third storyline in *Criminal* once again find Leo in the lead role. "Leo and the main character in 'Lawless' are two of the main characters who will be in most of the storylines, although there is another character that is alluded to throughout the first storyline. I don't want to reveal how exactly, but there's a running thing thoughout the comic that helps tie it all together, which you'll see in the first issue."

Readers of *Criminal* will want to pay close attention to all of the conversations in the book and things that happen in the background. "There is nothing in the book, no single line of dialogue, that is thrown out that doesn't actually mean something, that isn't part of sort of building the world," Brubaker said. "If you hear two people talking about someone in the background in a scene at some point, you're probably going to meet that person.

"I want it to be a comic that rewards its readers for buying it and I also want it to engage people," Brubaker continued. "I want it to challenge them in some ways. I want you to have to go back and reread it and go, 'Oh shit! I didn't notice that!' I've been trying to do that on all my stuff as much as I can, but there's always the fine line you tread of trying to tell a story really clearly so readers don't stumble and also giving them something with dual meaning and some kind of challenge where they go back and reread it and go, 'Oh! There was a clue about this!'"

"But there is a bar that all these characters go to that has a lot of history and a lot of the backup stories center around the bar," Brubaker continued.

"Sean and I have talked about, depending on how long the book goes and how long we get to keep doing it, doing single-issue one-off stories about various characters that we meet through the bar. I've already started mapping out the first one, which would be about the main bartender you see throughout the first arc; this grizzled, old ex-boxer. We talked about doing a story about him that takes place in the '70s or late '60s."

With *Criminal*, Brubaker hopes to take familiar noir genre tropes as ingredients and blend them into a potent and fresh story cocktail. "I'm basically trying to use the noir and crime genre in a way that plays with the clichés," Brubaker stated. "There's reader expectation with any sort of genre trope or cliché, so you can actually play off that expectation by sort of twisting the clichés in different directions. That's one of the main things that I wanted to do with this book and why I wanted to do the book. It was to do the kind of crime stories that I felt like I wasn't really seeing. The kind of stuff that when you start to describe it, it sounds like ten other stories, but when you read it it's much more of a character piece and goes in different directions than you would expect."

Criminal will focus on dark-toned noir and crime stories, but that doesn't mean the series won't have its share of lighter moments as well. "There is a lot of humor in it, actually," Brubaker said. "There is sort of a mood to it. I don't know exactly how to describe it. It's that sort of dark mood, but it does sort of have a more playful energy to it. When I was working on the first issue, I found that if I could get the mood of the book and the world across that I would have succeeded in what I was trying to do. I found that I had to start listening to a lot of smoky barroom kind of music while I was writing the first issue; going back to stuff that I hadn't listened to in years like Leonard Cohen and Tom Waits and even Frank Sinatra. I was trying to fit the right mood to it. It's got a sort of bleakness to it. I wanted it to feel sort of the same way inner-city America feels when you go there. It feels kind of bleak and depressing."

Each issue of *Criminal* will be jam packed with content including dark-toned crime stories, backup stories, and the occasional article. "Me and some friends of mine who are writers and comedians are writing a variety of things about the crime and noir genre and crime comics and crime movies," Brubaker said. "I'm writing an article about *Out of the Past*, which is an old Robert Mitchum film that's one of my favorite movies and I think is one of the ultimate noir movies. It has just about everything. It has the best femme fatale of all time.

"Patton Oswalt is going to write some articles about old noir films," Brubaker continued. "Patton is probably the biggest noir film buff that I ever met, even more than me. He lives in LA and he goes to these festivals where they'll show stuff that hasn't even been shown in theaters since the '50s and is not available on DVD or laser disc or anything. He'll go see a movie that you've been reading about for like twenty years. So he's going to write about that.

"I have other friends and I want to do a variety of things and make it some ways almost like a magazine," Brubaker said. "I don't want the text stuff in the back to just be a letters page, but we'll probably run the odd letter here and there if we get a good one. I really want it to feel like you're getting a complete package and you're getting your money's worth every time."

For those of you hoping to get the complete package, you'll want to pick up the monthly comics—those extras won't make it into the eventual traders. "So, if you want to get all the backup stories and extra material, those will only be in the comics," said Brubaker. "Instead of saving all the bonuses for later, we're giving the bonuses to the people who are actually making this possible."

Brubaker hopes that many people pick up *Criminal* and make it possible for the series to continue for a long time. "I could do this book for the rest of my life," he said. "And I think Sean could, too."

Brubaker's Noir World

MARK RAHNER / 2006

Originally published in *Seattle Times*. 4 October 2006. Web. Reprinted by permission.

You wouldn't notice Leo Patterson if you bumped into him on the street. But later, you might trace your missing wallet back to that anonymous bump.

Like a true criminal, Leo's goal is to be wallpaper. Nothing flashy. Don't deviate from a plan. Don't break the rules. Cut and run, to use a familiar phrase, if things start to go south.

You might not recognize Ed Brubaker if you ran into him on a Seattle sidewalk either, unless you're a hard-core fan of the prolific comic-book writer's hard-boiled work. Unlike his character, Leo, Brubaker's got a profile that's rising by the month, and it won't be long before civilians (read: *non-geeks*) can pick him out of a lineup.

Following a stint at DC Comics that included *Gotham Central* (an *NYPD Blue* take on a precinct of regular cops in a superhero world), a revamp of *Catwoman* and the outstanding *Sleeper* (about a tough double-agent with pain-conductor powers), Brubaker's been doing knockout work on flagship Marvel titles—*Daredevil*, *Captain America*, and *The Uncanny X-Men*. This week, he parlays that juice into a fairly risky venture of his own: *Criminal*.

The new monthly title (featuring art by Sean Phillips) is notable for being a straight crime story from Marvel, a company not known for venturing far beyond muscular dudes in tights; for being one of the few titles from its "Icon" imprint of creator-owned work by marquee talent; and for getting off to a smart, seedy start in its premiere issue.

"I wanted to do sort of the ultimate *noir* comic without being as over the top as something like *Sin City* is," says Brubaker, thirty-nine. "I mean, *noir* is essentially over-the-top and cliché, but I like the idea of taking those clichés and those genre tropes and sort of twisting them around."

In *Criminal*, Leo the pickpocket is also a master heist-planner who gets pulled into doing a job by crooked cops. He takes care of his smack-addicted, Alzheimer's-ridden mentor. And he's got a reputation around town: He's a coward.

Sitting in the book-crammed basement office of his Capitol Hill home, Brubaker explains, "It's more of an exploration of being a coward and of violence in the world, and through the story of this heist gone wrong, of exploring this person's reaction to the violence that's inside himself that he's kept bottled up all these years out of the need to be safe—and then what happens when he's pushed beyond the limit."

Brubaker's made his bones by infusing a darker, police-procedural element into mainstream comic books that's made them less preposterous to increasingly sophisticated/jaded readers—to his credit, even making the potentially cheesy and jingoistic *Captain America* a crackerjack espionage thriller.

"I think I have a fairly good eye for crime," Brubaker says.

And a past with a fair share of it. Much of it's chronicled in his semi-autobiographical 2001 graphic novel, *A Complete Lowlife*. Among some of his readers, Brubaker says, "There's a mystique around the fact that I actually in my teens and early twenties lived kind of a shady life, that I was involved in drugs and crime." While he's not anxious to get into a lot of details at this late date, he says, "I'm not ashamed of having survived it. I've spent some time in the felony tank, let's put it that way. That really straightened me out, as far as scared straight goes, like not sleeping while you're in a downtown San Diego county jail with, like, fifty other guys in the tank, getting legal advice from a guy who's covered in blood from getting beaten by police. That was lovely."

Adding to said crooked mystique is that Brubaker's a relatively large 6 feet, 200 or so pounds. There's also the now-infamous event some years back in which he arm-wrestled about fifty *Sleeper* fans at a book-signing—the losers having to buy a copy and the eight winners getting theirs for free.

But in fact, Brubaker's an affable guy far removed from his brutal characters, with an infectiously ear-splitting laugh and a soft spot for his stubby-legged wirehaired dachshund, Watson, and his codependent cat, Cromwell.

"Basically, you just grow up at some point," he says. He married his wife, Melanie, in 2000, bonding over their love of pop culture and science fiction, he says. A moment of crystallization occurred when Mel took his side in an argument with a friend over whether *Beneath the Planet of the Apes* was a lousy movie. (They maintain only the first ape flick is any good.)

His crimes and misdemeanors on the comic page in recent years have included messing with some long-established characters—for instance stirring up *Captain America* readers by bringing back Cap's long-dead young partner, Bucky, as a brainwashed Russian cyborg assassin called "The Winter Soldier."

"I do have a reputation for coming in and doing shocking things and shaking things up," he admits.

The Cap he always liked is a "sort of morose espionage comic, where it's this really depressed man out of time who's fighting against the hordes of HYDRA, and it's somewhere in between a superhero comic and James Bond or something, but with this dark, noir way of telling the story."

When Brubaker took the reins of blind hero *Daredevil* a few months ago, he made the already gritty comic downright ferocious—by putting alter ego Matt Murdock in prison and daring to keep him out of costume for several issues.

"I thought what you do is, you up the stakes. You take that car that he's (metaphorically) flipped over and flip it over a couple more times, basically. What if instead of just Matt having this problem with people knowing he's Daredevil—he's been outed by the tabloids, the government's after him for being a vigilante—I thought the worst thing that could happen is he gets thrown into prison with the Kingpin and Bullseye and all these people."

He shook up the X-Men by adding a sinister backstory to the current group's decades-old origin in "Deadly Genesis."

"My feeling is, I try to be true to the spirit of the early days of Marvel when I work on these books," Brubaker says. "Which is, for the first ten or fifteen years, you just had no idea what the status quo of these books really was going to be. They would feel like they had a status quo, but if the Thing quit the Fantastic Four, you'd feel like, yeah, eventually the Thing's going to come back, but he could be gone for *years*. You never knew what they were going to do in those books."

Sometimes the shake-ups freak readers out, but it needs to be done, he says. "It's better to get a reaction from people. It's better to do the kind of stories that you'd actually like to read yourself than to just worry too much and be too precious about the properties. What's interesting about the Marvel characters is that they were created to be broken."

Ed Brubaker Interview

DUANE SWIERCZYNSKI / 2008

Originally published in *Crimespree Magazine* 22 (6 March 2008): 54–57. Print. Reprinted by permission.

Ed Brubaker makes me wish I had a time machine.

I want to send him back to, say, December 1950, dead broke, with nothing more than a typewriter, ream of paper, and the address of Gold Medal books editor Richard Carroll. Then, I'd just sit back and wait for him to conquer the world of mystery paperback originals.

There's no doubt he would conquer, because Brubaker has the mad genius and the pedal-to-the floor work ethic of the best of the 1950s guys. Right now, Brubaker's responsible for no fewer than four of Marvel Comics' hottest superhero titles (*Uncanny X-Men, Captain America, Daredevil,* and, along with Matt Fraction, *Iron Fist*), but also *Criminal,* the Eisner-Award winning crime series, for Marvel's Icon imprint. And while *Criminal* taps into that sweet ultra-hardboiled Black Mask/Cain/Hammett/Stark vein, what makes the series a must-read is the undercurrent of strained and broken relationships—father and son, brother and brother, man and wife—running throughout the story arcs. Brubaker's characters bleed like crazy, but that's nothing compared to the heartbreak they endure.

So if I can't hurl Brubaker back in time, the next best thing I can do is pin him down for a few questions.

This Q&A was conducted over a series of emails. I'd lob a question, he'd smack it back at me. Then, halfway through, he shot a few questions my way, too. We'd double-back and pick up a thread from an earlier email, and . . . well, if I just ran the emails straight, they'd be confusing as hell. So I've reordered the sequence of questions a bit; I didn't change a single word. I just wanted to avoid this Q&A sounding like two rambling winos in an alley, mumbling about crooks and pulps and movies. Not entirely sure I succeeded, mind you.

Duane Swierczynski: When did you first get the idea for *Criminal*?

Ed Brubaker: The stories that I'm telling in *Criminal* have been bouncing around in my head for a long time, probably. "Coward," the first book, started as an idea for a graphic novel for a French publisher, back in 2002, or so, but we could never get on the same page about what it should be, so I dropped it. But it just kept fleshing out in my head over the years, wanting to be told. Then about two years ago, I was trying to figure out what Sean Phillips and I should do as our next project after *Sleeper* finished (that was our book at Wildstorm, about a double-agent left out in the cold), and it just occurred to me that I should create an umbrella title to tell any crime story I wanted to in. And so I started jotting down all my ideas for the stories I'd tell, and the characters, and it all came together from there and just started building.

DS: Did you intend the same thing for *Scene of the Crime*, back in 2000? I could see different kinds of stories playing out in that universe, too.

EB: *Scene of the Crime* was meant to be a continuing series of stories, but Vertigo kept changing the plan on us. First it was going to be a contract for three arcs, then two, and finally, they played it safe and just gave us a contract for the one we did. Then by the time they decided they wanted a sequel, Michael Lark (who draws *Daredevil* for me now) was deep into a Batman graphic novel, so it was never really going to happen. By the time he could have done it, it seemed like too much time had passed, and Greg Rucka and I had come up with *Gotham Central*, our cop book at DC, and wanted Michael for that. I had outlines for two more mysteries, one of which I've altered and hope to do someday as a novel or a graphic novel, or some combination of both, maybe.

Scene was my first attempt at writing a mystery and really sprung out of my love of Ross Macdonald's Lew Archer books, as a lot of first mysteries probably do. It also was something I came up with almost by accident, because our editor Shelly kept hounding me to pitch ideas to Vertigo and I couldn't come up with anything that felt much like what I thought they did, so I pitched something I would enjoy, that I thought for sure they'd pass on, almost just to get it done with, and strangely enough it got approved like the next day, and suddenly I had a writing career.

DS: How many *Criminal* stories do you have in mind right now? Can you see these arcs going on indefinitely?

EB: I have ideas for six or seven of them right now, but more keep occurring all the time. I'm actually delaying the third story I was going to do to write three interlinked short stories for the next few issues, that'll be longer than usual. Probably about thirty pages of story each issue for these. And they all take place in the late '60s to early '70s. One of them is the story of how Gnarly ended up owning the Undertow bar where all the criminals hang out.

But yeah, for now I could see writing stories like these forever. I see heists everywhere, as I'm sure you do, too.

DS: Since *Scene of the Crime*, many of your regular series have been infused with this great crime/noir vibe—*Sleeper* was pure noir, *Gotham Central* was hardcore police procedural, and so on. Is "crime" the lens through which you view much of life?

EB: Yeah, and espionage, a bit. My dad and his brother (who I'm named after) were both in the intel field. My uncle was a big mucky-muck in the CIA and my dad was in Naval Intelligence. Not that either of them were ever forthcoming with details about what they did, but it probably accounts for my interest in that genre.

And when I was a teenager, I was kind of a thief and a drug-addict. I did a lot of things I'm not proud of and lived in a really ugly world of speed-freaks and scumbags for a few years. Nearly going to prison straightened me out, though. Scared the shit out of me at eighteen, basically. But you never forget sitting in the felony tank with fifty other guys fighting over sandwiches.

So, when I started writing stories for other people to draw, I just always thought of crime stories. Just before my first paying work, in 1991, I had read a lot of the Jim Thompson reissues from Black Lizard and had been on a real true crime binge, so that probably played into it a lot. But I think on some level, I identify with criminals, even though now that I'm older and a homeowner, I hate them. I never liked any of the ones I knew, really, it was just the life I fell into. I like the ones I make up, but they're much more romantic than the criminals in real life.

DS: Very true. Especially bank robbers and heisters—they're guys you can cheer for, because they're just trying to beat the system. You mentioned reading a lot of true crime. What kind of stuff were you reading? Dillinger bios, or serial-killer-of-the-month paperbacks?

EB: More the latter, sadly. I was big into modern true crime then. *Zodiac*, *The Dead Girl* (about a murdered jogger in Berkeley and the necrophilia involved in her death), and one I can't remember the title of about the secret behind the Son of Sam murders. That one claimed there was a snuff-film ring that was actually doing the Son of Sam murders and that Berkowitz was only part

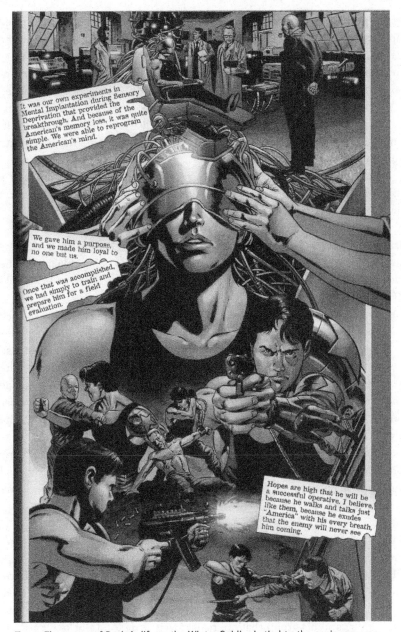

Fig. 9: The secret of Bucky's life as the Winter Soldier is tied to the espionage convention of the brainwashed sleeper agent in *Captain America* Vol. 5, #11. (From *Captain America* Vol. 5, #11 by Ed Brubaker and Steve Epting © Marvel; originally published by Marvel in 2005; available in *Captain America: Winter Soldier*)

of the group. It was a chilling read, whether it was true or not. It connected up to the murder of some movie producer who was found chopped up in the desert, too. There are some images in those books that I'll never get out of my head. I had a fascination with Ted Bundy books for a little while, too, for some reason. Then when I moved to Seattle, I was at a party once and realized it was in the house where Bundy took one of his early victims and I totally freaked out the girl whose bedroom that currently was by telling her about it. I'm like, oh yeah, wow, your bed's even in the same place hers was. I'm pretty sure she moved.

Now all the true crime stuff I read is about organized crime, or the police, or stuff like that autobio of the jewel thief that came out a few years back. I guess I outgrew the serial murderer phase, thankfully.

DS: Going back a second, those Jim Thompsons were among my first crime reads, too. I remember being broke in college, and only being able to buy one every so often. But each one I savored. Have you ever read Robert Polito's bio of Thompson?

EB: I never read that bio, actually. I meant to, but I was pretty broke back then, too. I was lucky enough to live in Berkeley back then, and Moe's Books on Telegraph generally got a bunch of used Thompson books in for cheap, so I was always trading in books and getting more of them. I think my favorite may be *Nothing More than Murder*, actually. It's about a guy who runs a movie theater and he and his wife aren't in love anymore, and he's going to leave her for another woman. It's a real tragedy, and I don't know why, but that one always stuck with me.

Another favorite that I read at that same time—the late '80s—is Fredric Brown's *The Far Cry*. That's one of the most messed-up books I've ever read and was a big inspiration to me. The writer obsessed with the dead girl genre has always appealed to me.

DS: What are you favorite espionage novels? I imagine you digging the old-school stuff . . .

EB: Probably LeCarré's *The Spy Who Came in from the Cold* is my favorite. I love all the Smiley books. And I really love Graham Greene's spy novels, too. I like to read nonfiction about espionage, too. There are a bunch of books about Kim Philby and his group that are really fascinating. And Rucka turned me onto the *Sandbaggers*, the old British TV show, which is so well written it's scary.

DS: Who are your favorite classic writers, aside from Thompson and Brown? (And by "classic," I mean people who are dead, and were producing stuff anywhere from 1930 to 1970.)

EB: I'm a big David Goodis fan, and Charles Willeford. Did you see the film they made of his book, *Woman Chaser* a few years back? That was really great. A truly bizarre work of art about art. I recently found an early '70s paperback original that I've been getting a lot out of called *Karate Is a Thing of the Spirit* by Harry Crews. I know he's not of that era, but I never knew he had his paperback original pulp writer phase. And I love Patricia Highsmith. Also, thanks to you, I recently discovered Dan J. Marlowe, who I can't believe I've never read before. *The Name of the Game Is Death* is one of the best books I've ever read.

DS: Who are you digging these days?

EB: The usual suspects, I'm sure. I read a lot of mystery and crime fiction. A standout for me the past few years, that I always try to recommend to people, though, is *About the Author* by John Colapinto. It's a really captivating book about the desire to be a writer, and the allure of fame and glory, and I don't want to say more than that, really. I just highly recommend it.

DS: You had an uncle who wrote noir screenplays as well, right? That's one hell of a genetic cocktail running through your veins. Did you hear little bits and pieces about what they did growing up? Or were you kind of oblivious to it until later?

EB: I knew my dad and his brother, my uncle Ed, actually, did something suspicious, because it was never talked about. I lived in Gitmo for three years, and started school there, and knew my dad was in the Navy, but I knew he didn't sail boats, you know? I have my Uncle Ed's CIA medal of service on my mantle-piece now, which I inherited when he died. Apparently it's really rare to have that, because usually those are kept locked up at Langley, according to an ex-spook I correspond with.

As for my Uncle John. He was John Paxton, married to my dad's sister, Sarah Jane. He wrote a bunch of movies. *Murder My Sweet, Crossfire, On the Beach, The Wild One* . . . the list goes on. He was always sort of an idol to me as a child, but mostly because he also wrote the cartoon *Emergency Plus 4*, the *Emergency* spin-off cartoon where Gage and DeSoto teamed up with four kids to solve crimes. Sadly, he died before I realized I was a writer and could have benefited from his advice. He was good friends with most of the Hollywood

Ten, but managed to get through the Blacklist era without naming names or getting in trouble, somehow, but I know that era soured him on Hollywood a lot. Dalton Trumbo's widow and my aunt Sarah Jane are still close, according to my dad.

DS: You've got to be one of the most disciplined bastards on the planet, because you produce so many monthly Marvel titles (*Uncanny X-Men, Daredevil, Captain America*) along with *Iron Fist* (with Matt Fraction), and of course, *Criminal*. What's your average writing day like?

EB: It really varies. Years back, when I first got to the four books a month level, I used to work five days a week from about 9 AM to 3 PM, making sure to get five pages a day done. Now, because of various distractions, I end up doing that a few days a week, and spending part of the weekend catching up on whatever I'm behind on. Sort of writing in spurts, on deadline pressure. I wish I was more disciplined, and I'm trying to get back to that all the time, but any time I have to take a day to go run errands and don't get any work done, it gets me out of the groove. It's really a constant struggle, and I often feel like a pulp writer, having to churn out a certain amount of stories a month to pay the bills. It's a good life, no question about it. It beats working a real job on its worst days, but it's a struggle that I feel like I'm always losing a little bit.

I always think I'd like to do less than I am, but then if I ever think about quitting any of my books, I can't. I just love writing them all too much.

DS: Every time I mention your name to a crime fan, he/she wonders aloud when you'll sit down and write a prose crime novel. Do you have anything cooking along these lines?

EB: I have, on and off. It's finding the time, really, more than anything. I write a comic a week for Marvel right now, just about, and write *Criminal* around all that. A few years ago, I got about halfway through a detective novel, but I had to set it aside to hit deadlines, and when I came back to it, so much time had passed, I couldn't get back into it the right way. But I do have a new one I started earlier this year that I'm sort of picking at a few times a month that I hope to actually keep working on. I need a deadline of some kind, is the problem. I've been making a living writing comics for so long that that eternal deadline cycle really motivates me.

DS: Any hint of what it might be about?

EB: When I was a teenager, my friend and I committed a pretty serious crime, and I got lucky, but my friend didn't, he got caught. It's something inspired by thinking about the various different ways that could have gone. I don't want to say more than that, because you know, if you explain your idea, you don't end up needing to write it sometimes.

So, let me turn this interview back on you for a while, since I'm curious. You've recently started writing comics. So, as a journalist and novelist, how are you finding the transition? People often compare comics scripting to screenwriting, but I always think comics scripts are like writing pulp poetry. You get paid by the page, you have deadlines to hit, and you can only fit so much text on any one page, so you have to keep it clean, but still make it feel like something. Still have a personality. When I write prose, which I don't know if I'm any good at, really, the one thing I notice is the freedom. The room to go as long as you need to. Even with *Criminal*, where I don't stick to a page count, I have to keep the narration really sparse because there's seven to nine panels a page.

So, how are you finding it?

DS: The transition's been a lot smoother than I would have thought. Before Axel [Alonso] showed me a bunch of sample scripts, I had only read a few— namely, Alan Moore and Neil Gaiman scripts, which were hyper-detailed. So it was really a revelation to see other scripts that were stripped down like movie screenplays: mostly, direction and dialogue.

But I think you're right: there is an element of pulp poetry involved. You've got to pack a lot of meaning into very few words.

Reading the sample scripts also made me realize that a lot of good scripts can be understood (almost completely) through the dialogue. But it's the art and art direction that bring it to life, set it in motion. Granted, at this point I only have five scripts under my belt. And I still try to fit way too many panels on a page.

EB: You can comfortably fit nine on a page, depending on your artist and what's supposed to be in each panel, but that's something you probably need to build to still. That'll come when you and your collaborator start to really groove together. That's the best part of writing comics, in some ways, those developing collaborative partnerships. Most of the artists I work with make me look so good at this point, because we know each other's style and intentions so well.

DS: But my natural style seems to be "stripped down" anyway—I really admire the James M. Cains and Ken Bruens of the world, who pack so much heart and muscle into so little.

EB: Yeah, that's something I'm always trying to get better at, making a really simple sentence have impact. It makes you appreciate Hammett and Hemingway all the more.

DS: What's your approach to dialogue? Any tricks you've picked up over the years on how to convey, say, emotion without being maudlin or wordy?

EB: I've never thought about it, really. Until this moment. I think I just try to make it sound realistic, but artistic, too, if that makes any sense. I generally cut a lot of dialog before I send in the final scripts, too, because I'll read some that just makes my eyes hurt, so that goes. It's like that line from Steve Martin's *L.A. Story*, where his friend says her policy on fashion is she turns her back to the mirror, then turns back around, and the first thing that she notices, she takes off. That's how I am about dialog, if I notice it, it goes. That's one thing I've learned well in ten plus years of doing this, to cut the fat. Again, that's something that comes from trust in the artist. A lot of the stuff I do in *Criminal*, I couldn't do with another artist. I know Sean can get facial expressions and mood across. I know he'll pace stuff properly so the story beats are right.

DS: Funny you bring that up. Lately, I've come to realize that I'm at my best when I have limitations—where I intentionally make my world a little smaller. In *Wheelman*, it was writing about a character who couldn't talk. In *The Blonde*, I decided: okay, no guns in this novel. There's Kowalski with a rifle in the very beginning, but once he puts it down, it stays down until the end. And in *Severance Package* (my next one), I gave myself another limitation. Don't want to tell you—it might spoil it.

But these kinds of self-imposed handicaps force me to be a little more creative with the characters and plot, and keep me away from lazy writing.

EB: Constraint-driven pulp fiction. I like it. Next time you have to write a mystery without the letter Y in the entire book. You know, I didn't even notice that in *The Blonde* there were no guns, damn. I did that to myself with the second arc in *Criminal*, "Lawless." It's a five-part story, and in each part, there's at least one heist of some kind. I thought I was going to have to break the rule for part four, but without even thinking about it, I suddenly had multiple heists going on in a flashback sequence.

DS: You talked about getting into a groove with an artist. But you also do your fair share of collaborations with other writers—first with Rucka on *Gotham Central*, and now with Matt Fraction on *Iron Fist*. How do you like it? How different is it from doing all of the lifting on your own books?

EB: It's the same and different. With *Gotham Central*, Greg and I had figured out a way to work where we never stepped on each other's toes. We'd
alternate storylines, and then team up for a "red ball" case every third arc. It
worked out beautifully all three times we did that. We'd talk on the phone and
hammer out the ideas, kick stuff back and forth and come up with new twists.
Then Greg would send me a scene by scene breakdown for the issue, with the
scenes divided equally based on whose characters were in each one (we wrote
different squads, mostly) and we would race to see who got his half in first.

With *Iron Fist*, it's a different ballgame. Me and Matt talk about the overall storyline, which I'm sort of steering, like I'll say, "When he goes back to
K'un-Lun, we'll find out there are six other mystical cities like this with their
own champions, and we'll stage the whole arc around a huge Kung Fu tour-
nament." And then Matt actually comes up with the names and ideas for the
champions and the new cities, and sends those to me for feedback. Then we
hammer out a plot for the issue, Matt writes the rough draft of the script and
I edit and rewrite and tweak. Then when the book is drawn and lettered, we
each go over and rewrite little things here and there, because often our artists have drawn something that makes our writing superfluous. So we cut it,
or change it. It's much more a fluid beast, *Iron Fist*. We're actually going to be
doing the next batch of issues more *Gotham Central* style, though, just to try
it out, and because I want to write more scenes on my own in the book. Often
on *Iron Fist* I feel like an additional editor as much as a writer, and that's kind
of weird.

Interview with Zoe Bell and Ed Brubaker

JOSHUA COHEN / 2009

Originally published in *Tubefilter*. 5 March 2009. Web. Reprinted by permission.

Here's an easy guide to judging the entertainment value of a web series:

- If the plot revolves around the psychosomatic effects of a knife that looks comfortable in the hands of Paul Hogan entering the heroine's brain, it's going to be good.
- If said heroine is played by a New Zealand stuntwoman whose beaten on bad guys, and broken vertebrae while standing in for leading ladies like Lucy Lawless, Sharon Stone, and Uma Thurman, it's going to be great.
- And if the knife-to-skull concept and subsequent assassin-with-a-conscious conceit is all conceived by an Eisner Award–winning comic book writer and filmed with a RED camera, it's going to be awesome.

So, yeah, *Angel of Death* is the most entertaining web show I've seen since I first heard Neil Patrick Harris sing about wonderflonium.

Created by the Ed Brubaker (who's credited with helping revive the crime comics genre and according to one fan, "manipulates crime fiction like Stephen Hawking's does time and space"), starring Zoe Bell (who's garnered cult celebrity status from a career as a stunt double to the stars and starring in Quentin Tarantino's *Death Proof*), and with a budget that numbers just under $1 million, *Angel of Death* is the story of how assassin Eve (Bell) suffers a serious head trauma that awakens an intense desire for revenge and an array of human emotions that assassins aren't supposed to have.

Brubaker's comic book pedigree easily translates to online video with tightly packed installments of equal parts kick ass and intrigue. Paul Etheredge should be given credit for bringing what is essentially a graphic novel to life without use of the now hackneyed Frank Miller/Robert Rodriguez aesthetics (though there is some Ang Lee). And Zoe Bell needs major props for playing a convincing killer with a newfound conscious, and bringing sweet action scenes to the world of web video.

I recently spoke with Ed Brubaker and Zoe Bell about how *Angel of Death* came to be, the transition from comics to web series, and the move from stunt double to leading lady.

Tilzy.TV: How did *Angel of Death* come to be?
Ed Brubaker: The producer, John Norris, was trying to option *Criminals* from me to do the web thing. I didn't want to do that for a variety of reasons. Then he basically dangled Zoe Bell in front of me and said, "Well, we've been talking to Zoe Bell about doing something, and she's very interested in doing something for the internet."

I was a huge fan of Zoe's from *Double Dare*, *Xena*, and *Death Proof*. And I just thought, "Why don't we create something new for Zoe Bell?" The next day I turned in the pitch for *Angel of Death* and we were off to the races at the point. Everything went really fast. Zoe loved it. The producers loved it. Everybody at Sony was really into it. I went out to some meetings and three months later I was writing a script and three months later we were filming a movie.
Zoe Bell: My manager at the time, Brent Calson was in contact with Sony and they were talking about doing some online, webby type stuff. I went into meet with them and it sounded cool and I said, "Keep me in mind." Then maybe a year later they sent through the synopsis of *Angel of Death*. It really tickled my fancy and I asked for more information and I came in for a meeting and Ed Brubraker was on the phone. We talked about it and it seemed like we were all on the same page and we were all excited about it. It's great when that happens. So we were like, "F#@% it. Let's make it happen."

Tilzy.TV: What's the basic premise?
Bell: Basically it's a feature film that's split up into chapters and those different chapters screen as webisodes.

The actual film is pretty much based around a woman called Eve who's an assassin, who's been trained to be void of emotion, and highly skilled with weapons and her hands. She suffers a fairly significant trauma very early on in the piece. It sort of shakes her up a little bit and she starts suffering from consciousness, guilt and remorse and all those pesky emotions. The rest of it is sort of her battling with what that means, and who she is, and how she fits in the world, and how to make it right . . . which includes a lot of ass kicking.

Tilzy.TV: Zoe, you've done stunts for a lot of bad ass characters. Are you channeling any of them when you're playing Eve?

Bell: I hate to sound like an actor wanker, but I'm really channeling Eve.

She became a very real character to me. I sort of wrote a history on her and she took on a life of her own. I think when I'm doubling people, I'm not aware of taking on the emotional side of their character. I'm sure I do on some level, but it's more about the physical mirroring of the person I'm doubling, of the actress and the character. Where in this all the action was an extension of this character we created. She very much feels like a complete personality to me and I sort of feel strongly towards her, like she's an old friend.

Tilzy.TV: Zoe, did you have any say in the storyline?

Bell: That was all Ed. He wrote it with me in mind. He apparently was a fan of mine, so that was exciting, so he wrote the script based on and around me. But everything about it came out of his crazy little head.

Tilzy.TV: Ed, given the pacing of comic books I've often thought they can easily translate to web series. How was writing *Angel of Death* coming from the comic book world?

Brubaker: It really came in handy to come from comics. The trick of *Angel of Death* was to do something that's designed to be a feature but could be shown episodically as a web show, too. So, the trick was that each episode had to have a significant amount of story in it and be a fairly compact piece of entertainment that had a cliffhanger that sent you to the next episode. But then when the whole thing was done, to be edited all together seamlessly into a film, too.

I had to make sure that every ten or twelve pages was a really tight little chunk of story. Because of that we end up having a lot more story in a ninety- to one hundred-minute-long film than the average one has actually. Each chunk of it is so packed with stuff.

Tilzy.TV: So the idea from the get-go was that it was going to be packaged together as a DVD?

Brubaker: Definitely. It was designed to really take advantage of all aspects of the internet and DVD market.

Tilzy.TV: Aesthetically, there are some hints to comic books and panels. How do you decide when, where, and how those aspects are going to appear in the series?

Brubaker: That's mostly stuff they're doing in editing. I think they're trying to edit it so it feels like a graphic novel.

Tilzy.TV: Do you like it?
Brubaker: Yeah, I think it looks really cool. I love split screen stuff. I thought that was the coolest thing of the Ang Lee *Hulk* movie, actually.

Tilzy.TV: Zoe, have you always wanted to act?
Bell: No, I never had the goals of becoming an actor. I remember having this weird feeling when I was younger that I wasn't going to be *famous* famous but was going to be recognizable, but it was nothing I ever chased or was aware of wanting. It really didn't come up as a reality or possibility until Quentin threw it at me, really.

Tilzy.TV: So after your experiences in *Grindhouse* and *Angel of Death*, do you think you'll pursue more acting?
Bell: Definitely. Right after *Death Proof* I realized that I needed to think of it as a serious possibility. It really sort of freaked me out a little bit, the concept. It's daunting to want to take on the task of trying to have an acting career in LA. It's such a crazy town. There are plenty of super-talented people that never quite catch a break and a lot of not-so-talented people that do. That's a scary pool to jump into, ya know? *Angel* sort of did shift my thinking, though. I thought you could either commit 120 percent or bugger off, so I did it and I found it really satisfying.

Tilzy.TV: Ed, is there any question I could ask you that could somehow tie the death of Captain America into an article about *Angel of Death*? [Editor's Note: Brubaker penned the recent series that sent Steven Rogers, the original Captain America, to his final resting place.]
Brubaker: Ha. I don't know, how could you?

Tilzy.TV: I'm not sure, man. I've been thinking about it for the past hour and I can't come up with anything, which makes the journalist inside me sad.
Ed: I can't think of any connection.

Tilzy.TV: Does Zoe's character die at the end of *Angel of Death*?
Ed: Probably not. If she can survive a knife to the head, she can survive everything.

An Interview with Ed Brubaker

CHRIS MAUTNER / 2009

Originally published in *Patriot-News*. 12 March 2009. Web. Reprinted by permission.

Q: So tell me about *Incognito*.

A: *Incognito* is an idea I've been mulling over since we were wrapping up *Sleeper*. I often try to think of the inverse of an idea to see what would be interesting—if this idea is interesting to explore in one direction would it be interesting to explore it in the other? Look at a story like *The Shield*, where you've got a corrupt cop who's trying to save his soul. What if you flip that to the other side where it's a mobster instead of a cop? I think of things like that sometimes and try to see if there's a story in there.

Sleeper's about a good person who for his government goes undercover as a bad guy and slowly loses whatever moral compass he had and starts to realize that the bad guys and the good guys aren't that different in the ways that they act. And maybe doing bad things for the right reason is just as bad as doing bad things for the wrong reason. There's a lot of moral gray areas to explore there, so I was thinking, "What if you did the opposite, what if there was a bad person somehow forced into a situation where they actually either had to or ended up doing good things, but they're someone who has no moral compass, who looks down at humanity and ends up somehow through circumstance being forced to live among them and develop sympathy for them perhaps?"

That's where *Incognito* grew out of, trying to figure out, is there a story in that character exploration? Then I started thinking of it in terms of a noir story and suddenly I was "Oh, what if it's a supervillain living in witness protection," and everything started to come together from there. All my love of old pulp characters like Doc Savage and the Shadow started to come out. The idea of trying to do a story that's sort of a mixture between the modern superhero and a '50s noir story really started to appeal to me. I started thinking

"What if the pulps had never stopped? What if instead of crime stories and noir, the crime pulp stuff was mashed in together with Doc Savage and the Shadow and Operator Number Five?" What if they made noir-esque stories with these characters? Everything started building from that.

Q: Tell me a little bit about the main character and how you see him. He comes across as not the most likable character, and that's always a little tricky because you want the audience to have sympathy for him.

A: He's definitely an antihero. That's the story. It's the journey of a bad guy. He's an Eastwood type. It's that kind of character, Eastwood in *Fistful of Dollars* or somebody who is clearly an outlaw. And yet we'll start to see there's something about this person. I think by the end of the first issue you get an idea that this guy isn't just this antihero who looks down on everybody and feels trapped by this thing. You see some of the wounds this guy carries and how he became who he is. He becomes a more human character even by the end of the first issue, even though he does retain that hardened edge of a guy who was raised on the wrong side. I guess if you're raised on it, it doesn't feel like the wrong side.

Zach and his brother Xander were raised—they're twin brothers—and they were taken from a state adoption home and have no memory of it. They're earliest memories are of being experimented on by this mad scientist guy who was in this evil organization known as the Black Death. They were taking orphan kids and doing science experiments on them to try to turn them into supervillains, basically. He was a twin and he and his twin brother were major enforcers for this evil organization and at some point about three or four years ago something happened to his brother and he ended up turning on the people he worked for. Now he's living in witness protection, but everybody thinks he's dead. And he's on drugs that make him a normal person. They shut down all of the enhancements that he's been given.

Q: That sounds a lot like some of the characters and themes you've been exploring in your other books like *Criminal*. Certainly the idea of family, like the Lawless brothers in *Criminal* and even the Cap/Bucky relationship in *Captain America*.

A: There's some truth to that. We all have a few themes we explore over and over again as writers, whether you consciously know it or not.

One of the main things in this for me came out as an accident in that it occurred to me that the main character was a twin when I was thinking about the themes of the book, when I was fleshing out the ideas of the book early on. The word *Incognito* has so many different meanings. You're doing a story about people who put on costumes and run around but doing it in a sort of noir way—well, all good noir is at heart character studies with a plot taking place around them. You really build your whole story from the character.

So I thought, "Who is this character" and it occurred to me that a lot of what the story is about is a guy who doesn't exactly know what his identity is. He's living a lie. The person that he truly is is taking drugs and is living in this suburban Anytown, USA, kind of place working an office job and pretending to be someone he isn't. He's completely incognito and yet he puts on a mask and feels like this is who he is. Or maybe it isn't. There's so much about identity.

And it occurred to me "why does this guy go into witness protection" and then suddenly the whole twin thing came up. Identical twins have so much of their identity sometimes wrapped up in their twin. A lot of time they're really close friends and have mental connections and things like that. So the idea of a twin separated from his brother and everyone thinks he's dead and he's living this new life for the first time on his own, but everything about it is a lie. So it really gets to the heart of what the story's about in a lot of ways.

Q: It's interesting because your description also fits Clark Kent.
A: Does it though? He was raised to be Clark Kent. Going into witness protection is a lot different. (laughter)

Q: That's true, but—
A: "As a baby, Superman killed many, many people, but he was able to testify against Kryptonians and moved to witness protection in Kansas to be raised by an elderly family."

Q: That's my recollection of the story.
A: That's actually a pretty good story. If I ever get my hands on Superman . . .

Q: One of those Elseworlds tales—
A: Even as a baby he had full adult intelligence. That's a creepy story though. I like that.

Q: But it does sound like you're playing off the kind of wish fulfillment that a lot of superheroes provide. Especially in that initial two-page preview, where the lead is saying, "I'm better than all the other people I'm surrounded by."
A: Yeah, it is kind of the flip side of Superman/Clark Kent sitting there and

Fig. 10: Zack Overkill completes another part of his assignment and laughs at the absurdity of doing the "right" thing, recognizing the scripted nature of his words and actions in *Incognito: Bad Influences* #4. (From *Incognito: Bad Influences* #4 by Ed Brubaker and Sean Phillips © Basement Gang, Inc; originally published by Icon in 2011; available in *Incognito: Bad Influences*)

thinking, "nobody knows." This is him sitting there and thinking, "Nobody knows I could kill all of you and not care."

Q: Are you consciously going to be playing off of the traditional superhero tropes in that aspect?

A: I don't think so. I never consciously set out to do a parody of anything.

Q: I didn't necessarily mean a parody—

A: No, I know what you meant. But I don't think I'm consciously trying to reference any other superhero comics at least. There's little nods here and there to the pulps because when you do a story like this and you're creating the whole thing from the ground up, you have to do a little bit of world-building. My world-building was creating these pulp-hero characters from the '30s and '40s and they're not really important to the story at all, they're just background elements to the world. You may not ever see them in the same way there's tons of elements in *Criminal* that nobody ever actually sees. We referenced Sebastian Hyde a number of times before anyone actually saw him.

With *Sleeper* we did that thing where the characters all told their secret origins in third person which was a little play on the origin stories of characters and a little play on the way origin stories used to be told. I don't think that's what I'm doing. Who knows? It's hard to tell when you're in the midst of it. I'm deep into writing this project now. All I can think of is the character and the shit he's getting into. Obviously the point of the thing is to explore the gray area between good and evil from the other point of view. We always see that side of it, the good person doing bad things and how that affects you; on some level this is approaching that.

Q: You talk about taking part of things from the pulps and noir and superhero comics. What things are you consciously taking? Are there any genre tropes you're taking and how do you roll them up and keep them from bumping into each other, because they're different genres, or at least perceived as such.

A: It's kind of apocalyptic noir in this weird way. Noir isn't really a genre— People think of it as a genre, but the people who think of it as that, when they start to tell you what movies that would fit into that, don't realize how elastic that actually is.

A noir story, if there are rules to it, the main rule seems to be whoever your main character is, nothing good is going to happen to him. (laughs) And at the end of the story he may be dead. If he's narrating, he may be narrating on his deathbed. It's more of the way a story is told as opposed to what the story is. Many things that a lot of people consider noir could also be considered straight crime stories. A lot of people consider the Parker novels to be noir, but I just think of them as heist novels. Parker tends to live through all of them and there isn't a lot of tragedy involved in that process.

I think instinctively I've always brought that air of tragic noir element to whatever I'm doing. I'm trying to subvert some of the principles of that genre a little bit by doing this. It's kind of an experiment to take pulp and make up sort of an evolution of where these pulp-styled characters would have gone and how they would have affected a world . . . and also to try to tell it through this really character-driven noir story. So it is a little bit of an experiment, but I really like the elements of something like Doc Savage; I love the apocalyptic literature of pulp fiction with these characters, who were just sort of weird, crazy, vicious characters who were planning to destroy the world, and you had a guy like Doc Savage, who would take out whole organizations, and whoever would survive they would take back to their institute and carve out pieces of their brain so they wouldn't be bad guys anymore.

There was weird stuff going on in those pulp stories that comics sort of evolved from. As comics started being more and more for kids, a lot of that eccentric bizarre early atomic-age stuff just fell by the wayside. That's the kind of stuff I'm tapping into a little bit with *Incognito*. Just using that hard, crazy science edge to some of this world. Not as if I'm the first person by any means to explore the pulp roots of what superhero comics grew out of. Alan Moore started a whole line of stuff. But they weren't the first either. We wouldn't even have Batman if not for the Shadow.

Q: I talked to you back when *Criminal* first came out and I remember you saying how with *Sleeper*, because it was aimed at more traditional comic book readers, you were able to be a lot more experimental in your layouts and design. And with *Criminal* you wanted it to be very basic so that anyone could pick it up. What about with *Incognito*?

A: I think it's mostly pretty straightforward. With every project it seems like Sean starts to experiment a little bit with the way he tells a story or structures a page. With this one, my favorite art from him, maybe ever, is the stuff for *Incognito* because I love the way he's doing these no-panel borders, using the gutter space as negative space and hard clean balloons for the word balloons. Everything's very mechanical except for the stuff that's hand drawn by him.

Sleeper—he'll probably do a story like that again, with that kind of experimental storytelling, but I've seen what he's doing now with these odd panels that have these full bleeds. He's doing this thing where he'll make certain panels pop so they'll bleed to the edge of the page.

Q: Of course, *Criminal* has changed. Both of you have gotten a little more experimental.

A: Yeah, but we're still basically sticking to a three-tier grid. I can't remember who said it, but if you can't tell a story on a three-tier grid you can't tell a story. The first advice I remember reading in a book about experimental layout,

Fig. 11: As Jacob Kurtz's criminal tendencies become more apparent, Frank Kafka pushes him to be more of a stereotypical man in *Criminal* Vol. 2, #7. (From *Criminal* Vol. 2, #7 by Ed Brubaker and Sean Phillips © Ed Brubaker and Sean Phillips; originally published by Icon in 2009; available in *Criminal: Bad Night*)

when everybody was trying to do weird angle panels and imitate Neal Adams with all of his crazy storytelling stuff he did, and somebody pointed out that before Neal Adams ever tried that he made sure he could tell a story in six to nine panels per page. Learn the rules before you break them.

Q: Not to take away from any of the other artists you've collaborated with, but this is the third book you and Phillips have worked on and you seem to click together well. What do you think it is that allows you to work together so well?

A: I don't know. We're just on the same page about the kind of comics we want to do. I really feel like a lot of what I do pacing wise really fits most of my scripts; if you look at any of them, they have as much description of facial expression and what the character is feeling as they do with "in the background there's this and this." All my stuff wouldn't work at all if I didn't have artists that can really generate empathy from the readers for the characters. Sean just does that really well. We love a lot of the same comics and aspire to do things on the same levels as the books we really dug. A lot of times we're playing to each other. I feel like I'm writing this stuff to some degree for Sean because he's the first person that reads anything I write for anything I own.

Q: Is this going to be an open-ended story? Do you have a definitive end in mind? Or could this go on?

A: It'll depend. I know the end of this story. I've got the last scene written already. It came to me early on. It's definitely left in such a way that if someone were to want to, we could revisit this character or other characters in this world, depending on if I end up sticking with that scene. The plan right now is once we finish this to go back and do more *Criminal*. We're having a lot of fun. With *Criminal* especially we built up a pretty loyal, sizable audience of people who are clearly following us over to *Incognito*. And hopefully we'll pick up some more from *Incognito*. As long as people keep buying comics by us in enough quantities that we can afford to keep doing it, Sean and I will put out as many of them a year as we can.

Q: I was going to ask you how *Criminal* was doing.

A: It's doing really well actually. We're one of the more stable books on the market apparently. We've been doing about 18,000 an issue. That's advance orders. I think we're doing close to 19,000 on final sales. That's better than most books like that. I always want to reach more people and I feel like it's still under-performing, 'cause I still hear from people all the time whose stores buy three copies and sell out the first day so I always know they could be selling at least a few more. It's better than almost everything Vertigo publishes.

Q: I was going to say.

A: Yeah, other than *Fables*. From my side, once we relaunched with the new format and I think after issue two, the orders for issue three actually went up and in issue four the orders were higher than one even. And we've just stayed at that level. One issue I think was thirty copies less. It's insane to have a book where the numbers are the same every month.

Q: What about the trades?

A: They're doing really well too. We've sent the first one back for a second printing, and we're pretty close to selling out the first print run of the second trade. I'm just waiting to get some statements. But we're moving really good numbers, and mostly through comic stores. We're not really doing huge bookstore push because I handle all that stuff myself. Also we're in print in five or six other countries and our French publisher has gone back to print with the first book. We're coming out all over the world with this stuff. The more books come out the more they seem to feed each other. Every day I hear from more and more people who are just getting turned onto it, so it just seems kind of crazy, for two years and only seventeen issues.

Q: How many issues is *Incognito*?

A: Five issues and then we're back to *Criminal*. We're doing the next Lawless story after that. *Incognito*'s just five issues. We'll probably do more of it. We'll see how we like doing it the further in we get. So far I like it, which is surprising, because after *Sleeper* I thought, "Let's just do crime stories and not deal with any of the super-powered stuff at all." But it's a lot of fun to be back doing something like this with Sean where we get to flex some different muscles and have some fun within that genre. I like working in comics where you can do a story like that and a large part of your audience goes into it knowing what a supervillain is.

Q: Working for someone like Marvel or DC you're under these creative restrictions as far as what you can or can't do with the character. In your case I'm not sure that's true, because they always say they can't kill the character and you did.

A: I've gotten really lucky with getting away with murder, literally, on books but also I haven't slammed up against a lot of restrictions.

Fig. 12: Blending Captain America's WWII stories and "weird tales" to create a horrific past for the supersoldier in *Captain America* Vol., #12. (From *Captain America* Vol. 5, #12 by Ed Brubaker and Steve Epting © Marvel; originally published by Marvel in 2005; available in *Captain America: Winter Soldier*)

Things you can or can't say I get a lot; in terms of from month to month, it seems to change. There's never any hard or fast rule. You can say "damn" in a book but you can't say "damn" nineteen times on a page. Weird things like that.

I don't think I could do the work for hire stuff if I wasn't also doing original work. I think they feed each other at this point for me. I went a few years only doing work for hire stuff when I first started out at Marvel before *Criminal*. It just seemed like I was going to lose my mind if I didn't start doing some work that I actually had a stake in and felt like was important to me. I have a big stake in *Captain America* and *Daredevil*. They are important to me but it's a whole different thing when you create all of it from start to finish. You own it and it's your universe. It's not everybody else's too.

Q: You don't have to worry about tying it into *Civil War*.

A: But even that stuff, if you take those jobs at Marvel, you can't complain when somebody says, "Oh we want you to tie into such and such." I've been really lucky. People think that happens more than it actually does. I have editors who say, "Hey our book needs a boost, tie it into such and such a thing." I've been on that end at DC. I don't think I've ever been on that end at Marvel but I'm sure there are people who have been.

You're trying to tell the best story with someone else's character, and I lie to myself and make myself believe I own the Captain America part of the Marvel Universe other than Brian being able to use him in *Avengers*. But during *Civil War* Cap was in every third book and usually getting beaten up by the main characters. He probably got captured like nine times during Civil War. I'm the only one who didn't have him get captured.

You lie to yourself and tell yourself it's your character while you're writing it. You have to; otherwise you're not going to do a good job and give the readers their money's worth, which is what your job is to do. Make people want to keep reading these characters. That's a great fucking job. It beats flipping burgers, which I've done. It beats any job I've ever had because it's still creatively fulfilling. But doing your own stuff is even more fulfilling. (laughs)

I like both. I love *Captain America*. Ever since I was a little kid I've had these ideas that I would grow up and work on *Captain America*. I probably went a good decade or so without ever thinking about it, but the moment I got that phone call from Brian saying, "Hey is there anything you want to do? I know you're exclusive is ending soon," and Joe called me the next day to offer me *Captain America*. There was no way I was saying no. It's pretty cool. It's the same way I would work on Doc Savage or the Shadow if Marvel had them. I find if I go a full month without writing something that I'm doing—all the stuff is intended to be read and enjoyed by people but *Incognito* and *Criminal*, as long as I'm doing something that Sean wants to draw and that I'm really into. *Bad Night* is one of the best things I think I've ever written.

Q: I have to say, I thought that last issue was superb.
A: Thanks. I was trying to do one of those James M. Cain style things. Jason Star did a book called *Twisted City* that has the best last scene in a crime story that totally changed everything about the main character in his last moment. I didn't go for that.

It's interesting. I do read the odd review and I noticed until issue four's reviews, almost all online reviewers were thinking that Jake was having conversations with the Frank Kafka character throughout the whole story. If you read it, you can see that's not actually happening at all. In the first three parts of the story, up until the very last panel of part three, he never acknowledges Frank's presence at all. As a reader you can think he's just imagining what his comic book character would say or do because he doesn't interact with him. It's almost like it's a voice inside of his head, which is what you're supposed to think. And then you realize it is a real voice inside his head.

That was one of my favorite things I've ever worked on and one of the hardest things to write too. There's not a single scene in there that isn't important to the big conclusion. Even the first line of narration about the house burning down across the street comes back around. Everything comes back around. I feel really lucky to have a platform to do stories like that. The minute that sales started feeling stable, that sense of "Oh this is going to go away someday" went away. I started to feel like we have a fan base that is actually following what we're doing. I was always worried during the first ten issues 'cause sales would fluctuate where it would seem like we were doing really good and then the next issue orders would be down 2,000. I knew we were being underordered. I didn't think it was a bunch of "trade waiters" 'cause I kept hearing from people who could find part five of a five-part story. I think we stabilized 3,000 higher than we'd been selling on the last four issues of the previous run. I can't believe the same stores are ordering the exact same number every time. But maybe.

Q: I suppose in these times retailers can't afford to take chances on extra copies of anything.
A: That's why I'm really thrilled *Incognito* did as well as it did. It didn't do as well as I initially thought when we first announced it and everyone flipped

out. But that was a week before the economy started to tank completely. Or at least publicly tank. Bad time to be launching a new book. I keep reminding people not to flip out too much about the whole economy thing because: a) that will just make it worse and b) even during the Great Depression 25 percent of the country was still working. Don't automatically assume you're going to be in the other 75 percent.

Q: Right. It's just in the newspaper industry.
A: (laughs) Right. You guys need to get a bailout together. The problem is those stupid news media conglomerates that seem to think you're supposed to make a profit on journalism. Journalism is supposed to be a break even thing at best.

Ed Brubaker: Crime, Superheroes, and Comic Book History

KIEL PHEGLEY / 2009

Originally published in *Publishers Weekly*. 15 September 2009. Web. Reprinted by permission.

PW Comics Week: The simplest way to describe *Criminal* is that it's a straight crime comic. But slowly over the course of the series, you and Sean have been introducing a larger story about generations of criminals tied to one robbery in the '70s. How would you describe the larger concept?

Ed Brubaker: The hook is that there's no hook. [Laughs] I mean, honestly there's the back story of the characters who are interlinked. Every book stars a character who was a supporting character in a previous book, but I sort of took that from Elmore Leonard more than anything else. There is a big story that we're building towards that will probably run like eight issues or so, but I'm still not ready to tell that story yet. Really, the thing that I wanted to try to do with *Criminal* was to create an umbrella title where I could do anything—anything in the crime field or any kind of noir story. I wanted to create a book that was the kind of book I wanted to read—where in every story line, you can just pick it up at the beginning and start there. If you're reading the series and following it in order, there are Easter eggs for you, but basically you can pick up any volume and start it. I always joke that it's like [Frank Miller's] *Sin City*, except that if someone jumped off a roof and landed on a car they'd die . . . and so would the people in the car. It's a more realistic version of that kind of thing.

But it's more than that. *Sin City* was about taking the superhero conventions and putting them in a noir world. The capes were overcoats, basically. But what we're doing is creating our own world of noir and crime and exploring any kind of genre you can do within that field. Our first story was a heist story. Our second story was a revenge story. Our third story was some sort of arty, cryptic, Rashomon-style crime story. [Laughs] And our fourth one was the most twisted thing I've ever written, which was a paranoid rant on the whole "Postman Always Rings Twice" genre but adding a lot more craziness into it. It's just the book I always wanted to read, but unfortunately there's no great hook for it. There's no, "He's an undercover cop working for . . ." There's no super twist other than us trying to create the best crime comic we can possibly create.

PWCW: With the next arc, you move into an area that has been a little more well-traveled in comics: a mafia story. Plus, you're bringing back the character of Tracey Lawless who proved very popular in *Criminal*'s past. After experimenting with elements comics readers aren't used to seeing, have you reached the point where you can now use a recurring character to play around with what readers expect to see?

EB: Yeah. A little bit. Part of it is that each character like Tracey or Leo [from our first arc "Coward"]—after we do a sequel to *Incognito*, we're going to do a sequel to "Coward." Part of that is just creating these characters and wanting to come back and tell more stories about them. I read a lot of series crime fiction. Most of the crime fiction that is out there and popular is series fiction. Even with TV shows like *The Wire*, you want to see what happens to Jimmy McNulty next.

With this story, and one of the things I'm trying to do in *Criminal* each time is push myself further and try something different. When we sat down to do what became [our third arc] "The Dead and the Dying," I wanted to do three standalone stories that would link together and ultimately be a story about a tragic femme fatale. You rarely see the point of view of the femme fatale, and I wanted to try something like that. With [the fourth story] "Bad Night" I felt like I was going to have a nervous breakdown writing it because it was so different from everything I'd done, and it was so intense and personal. In this one, I'm trying to push myself further by expanding everything I've done in the previous ones and taking on three or four plots—even though we mainly follow Tracey. It's also a flip on the [police] procedural, which is something I really love. Like "Law & Order" or any kind of private eye fiction. It's still taking on that genre and doing our own twist with it. Tracey's clearly the most popular character and people keep writing me asking, "What's next for Tracey?" So this is like his detective story, except it's about a guy who has no idea how to be a detective, working for the bad guys.

PWCW: From your previous super spy collaboration *Sleeper* through *Incognito* through this, telling the story of a man on the wrong side of an equation seems to be something you and Sean enjoy doing. What's the attraction to those kinds of set ups?

EB: I like grey moral areas. With *Incognito*, it was about trying to sort of flip things, where *Sleeper* was like, "What if you're a good person forced to do bad things?" [*Incognito*] was about "What if you're a bad person forced to do good things?" With this storyline "The Sinners," Tracey is a guy who was trained by the military to kill people, but he mostly killed people who deserved it— or people who his government said deserved it at least. Now he's working for Mr. Hyde, and he hates being an assassin and won't kill anybody who doesn't deserve it. Suddenly, there are guys in town who are connected and who are starting to show up dead—drug dealers and higher-up guys in various crime organizations around the city where someone should have to order their deaths or give the OK. Nobody knows who's doing this. So Tracey's sent to solve this crime, and he finds out pretty quick that the people he's trying to find—he kind of approves of what they're doing. He thinks most of these people deserve to die. [Laughs] So he's kind of in a fucked spot in some ways. Is he going to turn these people over or help them? And putting characters in a fucked spot is kind of what writing is about.

PWCW: With the big *Criminal* Omnibus edition coming in November, you've got a third format for the series where the single periodical issues are essentially a magazine featuring all sorts of articles on crime fiction along with the comics, and the softcover trades present the stories in book form. With a big special hardcover, who is your audience? Do you think your fans are buying these stories multiple times, or are new folks going to pick this up for the first time?

Ed Brubaker: Probably there will be some people who buy it twice. With the Omnibus, it's sort of a limited thing where we set a print run on it. More than anything, I think it's something Sean and I really wanted. It's something of an art book where the art is reproduced bigger and it's on really nice paper with a lot of extras in the back. I have a feeling that about half the people who buy will be people who have bought the comics and the trades already and just want to have this really nice art book edition. I buy stuff multiple times all the time, so I'm clearly that buyer. [Laughs]

I always joke that *Criminal* and *Incognito* and all my Icon stuff are really reader supported. Kind of like PBS . . . I feel like the people who buy our book every month are the people who we're trying to reward with everything. I get emails from some of the same people now every time an issue comes out. It feels like less of a fanbase and more of an extended family of people who like all the same stuff as we do. *Criminal* the magazine is a hybrid of things. It's bigger than the average comic, and the back matter is a whole thing on its own. That's why we don't reprint that stuff in the trade book collections. Most of the articles that aren't written by me are done as favors from friends of mine who are crime writers or journalists. It makes *Criminal* the magazine a really cool thing that's different than anything else out there.

PWCW: On the superhero side of the equation, you're currently working on *Captain America: Reborn*, which has resurrected Steve Rogers two years after he died in a highly publicized issue of the regular *Captain America* comic. You waited quite a while for the comeback. How did you have to adapt your writing to work as an "event comic" outside the regular series?

EB: Basically, deciding to do it as an event and have Bryan Hitch draw it affected it a bit, but mostly what affected it was the timing. Marvel's *Dark Reign* story is going on now, and I always thought when we brought Steve back it had to be a full "taking characters from all over the Marvel Universe" story. You've got characters from the Avengers and the Fantastic Four in there and all sorts of supervillains. I always thought it should be a combination of a Captain America story and an Avengers story or a Marvel event. It's got to be a big thing. But really, what affected it were things like in the next issue we see the Thunderbolts, and that's affected by "Well, who are the Thunderbolts now?" or having Norman Osborn in charge of [super spy organization] H.A.M.M.E.R. When I first came up with the idea of Steve coming back, that wasn't going to be a part of it.

Really, the way the story is being told is the way I always planned to tell it, but when you start working with Hitch, it turns a different lever on in your head, you say, "How can I make this the biggest scene possible?" And when you get the pages back from him, he's figured out how to take it up another eight or ten levels. He's an amazing collaborator in that he adds so much to what you do. But basically the story is the story I'd set up to tell from the beginning. We saw hints of it issue #42 when the Red Skull and Arnim Zola were about to bring him back and Sharon [Carter] broke the machine and sent him skittering through time accidentally.

PWCW: The device you've used to bring Steve back—which involves him jumping through the moments of his own life—reminded some people of similar mechanics on ABC's *Lost* but with issue two things have started to get more complicated.

EB: Yeah, well comic fans can be knee jerk about things like that. People who didn't see *Lost* didn't think that. [Laughs] But it was one of those things where I saw the last season of *Lost* and I went, "Oh fuck!" I had this story planned out, and I had no idea they were going to be doing [Kurt] Vonnegut the whole season, but the way things worked out were totally different. Honestly, mine was a very direct riff on and tribute to *Slaughterhouse Five*—to take a World War II veteran like Steve Rogers and have him be unstuck in time. I even used the phrase "unstuck in time" and was very deliberate about it in issue #1 that it was a complete nod to Vonnegut with Arnim Zola saying, "Listen: Steve Rogers has become unstuck in time," and the very first line of *Slaughterhouse Five* is "Listen: Billy Pilgrim has become unstuck in time."

I was talking to [*Lost* co-creator and occasional comics writer] Damon Lindelof about this after everyone was saying, "It comes from *Lost*," and he said he got so much shit for ripping off Vonnegut. [Laughs] Apparently, most people who read my comic haven't read *Slaughterhouse Five*, which was forced reading when I was in high school. Ultimately, they're similar approaches to similar ideas, and I didn't formulate my idea because I watched *Lost*. I'm not going to change my plans because *Lost* did something similar . . . and with Steve unstuck in time you get to revisit classic moments and watch him struggle through his own life. For people who have just picked this thing up for the first time and haven't read *Captain America*, they can see that these are formative moments that shaped who this guy is and why he's a hero.

PWCW: How is the challenge of taking all those moments and fitting them into a time-travel story different from writing your other new book *The Marvels Project*? In that series, you have to look at the history of Marvel superheroes in the 1940s and rework all of that information into an espionage tale.

EB: They're totally different challenges, actually, because *The Marvels Project* is so much more of a sprawling epic whereas with Steve's story in *Reborn* you're finding eight or ten key moments from his life and have them seen through a new perspective. With *The Marvels Project*, it's more about looking at a huge history from all the stuff that was published in the 1940s and all the stuff that's been told about that period in modern Marvel and all the retcons [retroactive continuity, or revising a past comics storyline to accommodate a current plot] that have occurred. You have to take a lot of threads and ideas that weren't meant to be a part of the same universe or linked—for instance, how a lot of [former Marvel editor-in-chief] Roy Thomas's reign was about trying to find ways to make the 1940s characters link up with what was going on in the 1970s. He was telling all these weird stories to explain things like how *Captain America* was published in the 1950s even though Cap and Bucky were blown up at the end of the war. I'm taking all of that stuff and finding the stuff that makes sense as a canonical Marvel origin. It's different kinds of storytelling. *Reborn* is a Cap/Avengers slam bang whereas *The Marvels Project* really takes its time.

The hope is that this will be the project that stays in print forever. When anybody wants to know, "How did Marvel start?" you give them this book. It really does get into the blending of actual history, the comics of the '40s and our modern retcons and weaves a story amongst all of that. It's among my favorite things that I've ever done at Marvel. What an honor to be asked to write the official "This is how it all began" story.

Interview: Ed Brubaker

OLIVER SAVA / 2011

Originally published in *The Onion, A.V. Club.* 20 July 2011. Web. Reprinted by permission.

The A.V. Club: *Captain America* was the first big title you did for Marvel. How was Captain America offered to you?

Ed Brubaker: I had been on an exclusive contract with DC. I was just wrapping that up, and Brian Bendis, who I'd known since the early '90s, when we were both working in independent comics, was becoming a big writer at Marvel, and he'd been wanting me to come write something at Marvel. And I just kept staying at DC and doing *Catwoman* and *Batman*, and stuff at Vertigo and Wildstorm. He basically called me up and was like, "Come on. I've been trying to get you over here for years. What character could Marvel give you that'll get you over here?" And I said, "Well, I'd really like to write Captain America at some point, but you guys just hired someone for that." And then he said, "Oh no, no. That guy is actually not gonna stay on the book. That's an interim thing." So the next day, Joe Quesada called me up to talk about Captain America. And my big idea coincided with the one thing Joe was really hoping someone would do on *Captain America*, which was to bring Bucky back.

The reason I wanted to write Captain America was, I'm a military brat. I was a Navy brat. I actually started school at Gitmo. There's a military base there that officers, at least back in the early '70s, would bring their families there, and there were neighborhoods where you would live, and there's a school and stores. It's like a tiny American town on Cuba. This is back in the days when nobody talked about Gitmo at all. But when I grew up living in military bases and traveling around, comics was one of my main things as a kid. And I grew up surrounded by all these naval intelligence and Marines and all sorts of people like that, and for some reason just liked the idea of growing up reading *Captain America* comics in this sort of milieu. It really spoke to me.

Because he was a super-soldier. He wasn't, like, Superman or something. He actually was a guy who fought in World War II.

It was the kind of character that really appealed to me as a kid, and I always wanted to try to do a more modern version of that. Something that blended a . . . I wouldn't say "real-world feel," but I definitely wanted to try to make it seem more like 24 or James Bond or something. There had been a few issues that I got later in life that Jim Steranko had done. Those were always my favorite Captain America issues. It was, like, three issues. It really felt like his *Nick Fury: Agent of S.H.I.E.L.D.* stuff, but with Captain America as sort of an operative. I always thought that was the most appealing way to use Captain America. As some sort of cool Delta Force, special-mission kind of soldier. I had this idea about doing that, and I'd always been angry as a kid when I found out that Bucky dying was some huge retcon that they did because Stan Lee didn't want to have sidekicks. [Laughs.] So some part of me was always like, "You know, if I ever get to write *Captain America*, I'm bringing Bucky back."

It's kind of amazing that six and a half years ago, we brought Bucky back and people were furious. And now he's become one of the more popular modern Marvel characters. I can't tell you how many times I've had to shoot down people wanting to do side one-shots or miniseries about the Winter Solider, and I'm like, "No, no, no. That's my character. You guys can't go mining his history." [Laughs.] So it's kinda funny. It's pretty awesome, though, that he became basically the most popular new Marvel character, probably since Deadpool. You know, there's toys. I have toys made from this guy. That's pretty nuts.

AVC: In an interview you did with *Comics Journal* a couple years ago, you mentioned that the major themes of your writing are family relationships, personal relationships, and people not being able to escape their pasts. How have you found it different exploring those themes in your superhero writing vs. your more realistic crime books, like *Criminal* or *Lowlife*?

EB: Well, I mean, those are pretty broad themes. [Laughs.] I don't set out, ever, to go, "What's the theme of this story?" Everything I write comes from the character and what it is. The major difference is when I'm writing something that's going to be in *Criminal*, I don't necessarily ever have a moment where I e-mail Tom Brevoort and go, "I need a really big Marvel supervillain." Because I know I'm building all the characters and the world by itself, and I don't necessarily need these sort of James Bond setpieces. But whether you're writing a superhero action thing or *Die Hard* or a small character-driven crime story, all of it is the same writing, really. If you're doing it right, you're still plotting your story the same way, or you're still looking at this story through your characters' eyes, the same way as you would if it were any other story.

AVC: Your *Captain America* is political and grounded in real-world situations. Last year, there was the *Captain America* Tea Party mini-scandal, and this year, Superman renouncing his US citizenship got mainstream press. Do you think people should just be more accepting of comics as potentially political criticism?

EB: Well, I wouldn't necessarily say that they're criticism. They're not like editorial cartoons. With me, I didn't set out to do anything critical. I was just trying to tell a story, and it appears that there are certain elements in American political life where even portraying them at all is seen as being critical.

When I was a kid, during the time that Watergate was happening, in the *Captain America* comic, the supposed president turned out to be in league with a group of supervillains. And that was kind of how Marvel reacted to what was going on in the real world. And Captain America discovered, "Oh my God, my government is corrupt." And he quit being Captain America for almost a year. I remember reading that as a kid and being blown away by it. But the important thing with any Marvel comic is to remember, it's not our world. And when you're writing Captain America, the most important thing, at the end of the day, is whatever your story is, it's a superhero comic. It's never our world, specifically. Marvel feels a lot like our world, but it's always one step removed. The Nixon in the Marvel comic wasn't the same guy in the same scandal as the one in real life.

And the whole thing with the Tea Party getting all furious at us . . . I never intended it to specifically be the Tea Party. And I don't think that I was necessarily critical of anybody in that actual two-page sequence or whatever. I was trying to show that when you get outside of major metropolitan areas like New York City or Seattle, or any major city, when you get ten minutes outside and into the country, attitudes are completely different. That's very American, that experience. And that was what I was really trying to do.

And the thing that was interesting about that was: In Marvel, it's not Exxon oil, it's Roxxon Oil. It's always something different. It's not the Mafia, it's the Maggia. They're always one step removed. So that was the only thing that I was like, "Oh, shit. The letterer threw a sign in here that specifically says that this is a Tea Party rally." I wouldn't have done that, because it's one step removed: I would have called it the Coffee Party or something. Or, I don't know, the Patriot Party. Just something to make it one step removed. But suddenly it was this huge uproar, and I was getting death threats from people for . . . I guess just showing a rally in a Captain America comic, and having the Falcon say he wouldn't feel comfortable at an anti-tax rally in Boise, Idaho? A black guy from Harlem is not gonna feel comfortable in that situation. I was just writing the character as he's always been portrayed.

But the reaction to it was, literally, I was getting death threats for two panels of a comic book. How is that not like the Taliban or al-Qaeda? So that really shocked me. And that made me basically give up having a public e-mail or any way other than Twitter for people to reach me. Wingnuts, man.

And the thing is, I'm not some sort of hardcore political animal. I'm pretty moderate. So it's just kind of appalling that just because I say someone's an idiot on Twitter, suddenly I'm some sort of left-wing crazy. My dad was the head of naval intelligence, and my uncle was in the CIA. I'm not some sort of left-wing or right-wing kind of person at all.

AVC: You've said you wanted *Captain America* to be like a spy novel, and you seem to have different genre influences for your projects. For *The Immortal Iron Fist*, you took elements from pulp serials and martial-arts movies. *Catwoman* had a very noir feel. Are there other areas of genre fiction that you still want to explore?

EB: Honestly, at some point, I really want to do a romance comic. [Laughs.] That's the one thing. I've done crime comics, I've done sci-fi comics. I've done superhero comics. I don't like romance novels. I will watch the odd rom-com movie, and my wife makes fun of me for it. But romance comics, for some reason, really spoke to me as a kid. I don't know why. I think it was the John Romita art. It's too bad, because the only person I would really want to do a romance comic would probably be John Romita. But maybe I can get Butch Guice to draw it like John Romita instead. So yeah, it's something I've always wanted to do. I'm not saying I'd want to do a monthly series of romance comics, but I'd like to do a "tribute to romance comics" kind of thing. It's a genre I always thought was kind of cool. They're so funny to reread now. They're so over-the-top. It would be interesting to try to do a bunch of romance-comic short stories. To get Marvel to bring back *Modern Love* for a few issues and let me write it. With a big artist drawing short stories. Call it *Postmodern Love* or something. [Laughs.]

AVC: Your books have had a lot of male protagonists, but there was one book where you explored the feminine side of superheroes. What drew you to Selina Kyle and *Catwoman*?

EB: Well, that one started weird in that I liked her character from the old days. Back when she was a jewel thief who Bruce Wayne was in love with. And I loved all the Earth One or Earth A or whatever Earth they call it, where they have the All-Star Squadron, and Catwoman eventually retired, and she and Batman got married, and their daughter was Huntress. I remember all of those stories from my childhood, from getting old Batman collections from the '50s and '60s. And so I'd sort of had that early attachment with her as a character. And I liked this idea of a character who was this person who can exist on the streets or in high society, or is some awesome jewel thief, or just a badass. She seemed like the coolest comic-book character they had, in a lot of ways. And when I just started on *Batman*, Matt Idelson called me up and asked me what I thought of the Catwoman comic that was going on. And I had read the odd issue here and there and I felt like it was not living up to that potential. There was too much T&A.

AVC: Jim Balent—

EB: Well, not so much that, as much as just . . . Yeah, I don't want to call any names out, it's been so long since I looked at any of that stuff. I just recall thinking that I felt like both the writing and the art weren't letting the character be the character. They really weren't getting who I thought she could be. And I really liked the way Frank Miller portrayed her in *Batman: Year One*. I liked elements of that a lot. The sort of dominatrix kind of character who has this really tough upbringing. So I wanted to try to find a way to blend that Frank Miller *Year One* version of her history with the things I really liked in the Silver Age Catwoman character, who was more like a high-society sort of person. And Matt asked me what I thought of it, and I told him, and he said, "So, do you want to take over the book, then?" And I realized I had kind of talked myself into it through the conversation. And I just said, "Well, can we redesign her costume?" And he said, "Yeah." And I said, "Well, I'll do twelve issues, at least." And I ended up staying on it for almost forty issues, I think.

I got lucky enough to meet Darwyn Cooke before anyone knew who he was. And I got him to redesign Catwoman, and ten years later, that's the look of Catwoman. It was a lot of fun, though. And I really felt like we had established a good backstory for her as an orphan raised within the system who goes on to figure out her way through life, and be someone who can play the part of someone from high society, but who actually knows how rough it can be on the street at the same time. I'm really proud of a lot of stuff we did on that book, especially the stuff with Holly.

AVC: I especially loved "No Easy Way Out." Right after the big storyline where everything bad happens.

EB: And that was something that we never see in comics, it seems like. Especially back then. Like, eight or nine years ago. We rarely saw a comic where the whole storyline after a big thing happened was about the aftermath, and the effects this kind of violence has on people. Because we're always on to the next comic, and it's not a big deal. But Green Arrow shot an arrow through someone's eye last issue. [Laughs.] Or whatever. I'm being facetious, but basically, it just feels like these characters never have to deal with that kind of stuff. And if you've ever actually been in a fight, or seen any kind of hardcore violence go down, it's jarring. It stays with you for a while. So I wanted to do something that really dealt with that. And it's great that I got three issues of Javier Pulido to sort of be my aftermath guy.

AVC: I love how you guys showed Holly's drug addiction with the images in the bubbles.

EB: Oh yeah, the junkie vision. That might be my favorite single issue of anything I ever did at DC.

I loved using . . . I kept getting that spam e-mail from the Dalai Lama, where he was asking you all these questions. I was like, "Why is the Dalai Lama sending e-mail spam?" And this is the early days of e-mail for me. And it just occurred to me that I should use that somehow in a story. That each of these questions he says represents some part of how you feel about life, and should be the climax of a single issue about Holly.

AVC: On Twitter, you've mentioned that you're a *Batman: The Animated Series* fan. Did that show have any influence on your *Batman* run at all?

EB: Definitely. That was one of the reasons Darwyn and I had the exact same vision for who this character should be. Because he came from working on that animated series, and working on *Batman Beyond*. Honestly, when I first started getting published, I was writing and drawing my own independent comics, and I didn't actually have a clue I could write superhero comics. I had stopped reading superhero comics about six years earlier. I'd pick up the odd one, and it really wouldn't connect with me. This is during the period when Image Comics was just starting, and you'd pick those up and flip through them, and it just felt like they were all splash pages. And I didn't think anything was grabbing me. I think storytelling in comics has come a long way in the last twenty years in general, like mainstream superhero comics. Things they learned from the '70s and the '80s and things they learned in the '90s

Fig. 13: A view of the street and its criminals from the perspective of Holly Robinson in *Catwoman* Vol. 3, #6. (From *Catwoman* Vol. 3, #6 by Ed Brubaker and Brad Rader © DC Comics; originally published by DC Comics in 2002; available in *Catwoman: Crooked Little Town*)

about the widescreen, sort of splash style have all blended into things that are much easier to read now than they were in the early '90s. And much smoother to read than they were in the '70s and '80s, when they were completely over-written. The best comics out now are almost a completely different language when you put them next to comics from the '70s. The best stuff from the '50s onward is still amazing, but I go back and read comics from the '70s a lot for research, and it's just stunning how much they're overwritten. [Laughs.]

I think what happened was, I didn't have cable at the time, and I went to someone's house, and they had videotaped some of these Batman cartoons and showed them to me. And I was kind of blown away by it. It was the first moment where I could imagine writing a Batman story. I was like, "This is what I should do for a living. I should write stories like this. I could do a Batman comic if I could do something like this." Not realizing that would be really hard to do. And it took me six years to get to the point where I was writ-ing Batman comics after that. But that was the first moment where it even occurred to me that I could possibly do it. Anytime there'd been an opportu-nity before, I'd just think, "I don't have any ideas for Batman." But there was this specific episode where the Scarecrow goes after Batman and he has this nightmare-dream sequence, and I remember being really affected by that one. Where he sees his parents walking into the tunnel, and the tunnel becomes a gun, and the bullet fires out of it, and blood is dripping from the barrel of the gun, and I was like, "Holy shit! This is for children?"

AVC: Apparently, though, the blood in that scene was actually miscolored. It was supposed to be sand, and that's how it got past the censors. That scene is great.

EB: I got the complete set of that stuff last year, and I've been watching them here and there. For a while, it was hard to go back and watch the really early ones, because I loved the design they did when they brought the show back later, and everything was much more streamlined-looking. All the characters looked a lot cooler. Those early ones looked so much like they were going for that Fleischer Superman look. But now I really like those. I think there's a lot of really good stories in those. There's one in that second run that they did when they did the *Batman & Robin Adventures*, or whatever it was called. It was another Scarecrow one where Batgirl dies. That's one of the best episodes ever.

AVC: That's a really dark one.

EB: Yeah. [Laughs.] I know. That's why I was like, "I like this show." That was a big influence. When Bob Schreck first got the job in the Bat office, I'd been talking to him about doing some stuff, because I'd worked with Bob at Dark Horse. And then he told me he got the job at the Bat office and he was tentatively offering me a run on *Batman*, and I was like, "Well, can I do the Batman animated comic instead?" [Laughs.] Thinking that was the better job to have. And luckily for me, career-wise, that job was taken by someone else, and that was their steady gig. I did end up getting to do one issue of that when there was some fill-in they did. I got to write one issue of the *Batman* animated-series comic.

AVC: What was the co-writing process like on *Gotham Central*? You've done that for a couple books now. How does the work get divided, and what do you think having two writers brings to the story?

EB: Well, it's different with every writer you do it with. That's the problem with co-writing. Sometimes co-writing is practically just being an extra editor on the book. Sometimes co-writing is doing more than half of the work. And then sometimes it's pretty smooth and easy, where you evenly divide it up. With me and Greg [Rucka], we designed *Gotham Central* to be a book we could share without stepping on each other's toes or without having to check with each other or making each other read our scripts. Because sometimes reading another writer's comic script is more difficult than just writing your own comic script, because it's work. [Laughs.] They pay editors to do it. It's not always fun to read comic scripts. It's much more fun to read their comics when they're drawn.

So with Greg and me, we wanted to do a book where once a year, we could team up and divide up the work and do a big story, our red ball, basically, like from *Homicide* [*Life on the Street*], where it would be the big moment. And then between that, we would each get an arc that we could do that would focus on . . . He would do the night shift and I would do the day shift, or vice versa. That was how we came up with it. We decided to divide up the book between shifts. Because there was this great episode of *Homicide* that showed what happened in the homicide squad when our main characters all weren't there. They actually shared desks with the people who were on the other shifts. So we sort of took that as our inspiration to develop the MCU, which would have the twenty-four-hour police shifts in there. So we divided it up and took first shift and second shift, and that was really easy with Greg and me. I think because of the way we started out, we both came into writing superhero comics in the Bat office. I was a little bit behind him, but we both came from a real crimefighter sort of perspective. He was a crime novelist already, and I had done some crime-related mystery comics, and that was definitely where I approached my storytelling from. I was thinking of it as a crime story at that point.

We were working on an outline for this *Batman* event called "Officer Down." It was about Jim Gordon getting shot and retiring. That was a one-month-long or two-month-long event. And Greg and I were tasked with writing the beat sheet for the whole thing after we all sat in the room. I think I came in late on this, but somehow I got corralled into being the person who . . . Greg and I batted the ideas back and forth, and then we put them in, basically, the spine of the story, so everyone else knew what to write in their parts. And when we were working on one part that had [police detectives Crispus] Allen and [Renee] Montoya walking through this crime scene where Gordon gets shot, and we realized how cool it would be if we did a comic like this every month. Where it was always about a crime scene where the Joker walked through and killed a bunch of babies. Just seeing the horror from a perspective that . . . You don't see it from Batman's point of view. These people, they do this every day to the point that it becomes a grind. And how angry they must get, and feel powerless that they can't catch these people, but Batman's going to do it. And half of the time, they're not gonna get convicted, because Batman arrested them. Things like that. It just seems like a comic that really needed to exist.

We spent a couple of years trying to get DC to let us do it, basically. And by the time we got them to agree to do it, *Powers* had come out and become this huge hit. So we had an example to point to, going like, "Look! Someone is already doing this, and it's a huge hit! We're missing the boat here." So that's kinda how that came about. But Greg and I wrote really easy. I brought him on to help me on an arc of *Daredevil* just because I thought it would be fun to get the band back together. Because we had [illustrators] Stefano [Gaudiano] and Michael [Lark] and [colorist] Matt Hollingsworth. So I thought, "Okay, let me do, like, a legal thriller." Because Matt Murdock is a lawyer. Let's do "Matt Murdock has to save someone from death row." So we got on the phone, and it was just like *Gotham Central*. We came into it knowing what big beats we needed to hit, and then we'd need to figure out, "Okay, well what happens this issue?" We're on the phone for an hour, and by the time we're done, we've got most of our major beats figured out, and then we figure out who's gonna take which scenes. That's kinda always how it went. With *Gotham Central*, we'd take our character scenes, but we'd try to make sure each of us was doing exactly half of the issue. Or if I did one page more on an issue, he'd take one page more on the next issue instead. It was always very evenly balanced. So it was really, really easy.

Co-writing with Matt [Fraction] on [*The Immortal Iron Fist*] was pretty close to how Greg and I did it, at first. And *Iron Fist* was a book I had been really wanting to write. And Marvel wouldn't let me write it because I had too much on my plate, so they said if I wanted to do it, I had to bring on a co-writer. And Matt was just getting in at Marvel, and I thought, "Well, I'll do it with Matt, then." Because he was doing *Punisher*, and I know he was looking to do more comic stuff, and we were already friends. It seemed like he would have the right sensibility, so I asked him if he wanted to do it, and he did. And I kind of had bits and pieces of the first *Iron Fist* arc already figured out, and Matt had a lot of ideas about these women who would turn into cranes, and these villains who wanted maglev trains, and all this stuff that ended up becoming a three-arc-long storyline. So we kind of integrated.

I wanted to do a story about the guy who was the Iron Fist before Danny Rand. That was the thing that always bugged me about Iron Fist. The thought that Danny Rand was the only one, somehow. Yet they had this costume, and this legend of this person who would be the Immortal Iron Fist. I'm like, "Well, these guys are all a thousand years old, and they have this Immortal Iron Fist costume sitting there. There had to have been previous Iron Fists." That was my main thought on that. "Okay, well, we need to do a story on the previous Iron Fist, who, it turns out, didn't actually die." And so Matt and I plotted out the first six issues pretty tightly together. And for the first issue, we divided it up pretty evenly. And then once it was done and lettered and everything, we did a pretty major polish over the lettering, because we had just written too much stuff. I think we were both trying too hard to make sure it was . . . You'd have to see the non-published version and compare it to the published version. We made some mistakes that you can make when you're co-writing, where you each accidentally write some similar stuff.

But for the most part, it went pretty smoothly. And after the first arc, and even toward the end of the first arc, Marvel was really pushing me to step away, and Matt didn't really need me so much. So I was co-plotting, and then I would pick certain seasons to write or rewrite. And all the way through issue 14, from that point on, Matt always wrote the first draft, and then I would go in and tweak stuff or rewrite a few scenes. Certain stuff, I would just take. And when Matt's first kid was born, there was an issue where we divided up the scenes, and I wrote half and he wrote half, and then I sort of polished everything and made it all fit together perfectly. Because that's the thing about co-writing: When you do break up the scenes, when you put them all together . . . Like with Greg and I, we'd plop a thing out, and then we'd have the beat-by-beat outline, and we'd kind of race to see who could finish their half first. And if you finished your half last, you had to be the one to make all the scene transitions look good. [Laughs.] So whoever finished last got to do the cleanup.

I think the issue of *Iron Fist* I'm the most proud of is the one I didn't have anything to do with at all. It was Matt's last issue and [David] Aja's last issue. It was the epilogue issue. The one that ends with Danny's birthday. I just love that issue so much. It was everything I always wanted the *Iron Fist* comic to be, and I didn't have anything to do with it other than reading the script and going, "Hey, great job!"

That was an odd thing, because I always worried that Matt felt like people were giving me too much credit, but at the same time, I felt like, "Well, I want some credit." Because I did work on stuff. That can be a problem with co-writing. I was a much bigger name than Matt at the time. And reviewers would credit me with something he'd written. What was weird was, working with someone like Matt, who has a really good sense of humor, and would write really oddball dialogue sometimes, that will bring out that part in you when you're working with him. So there were specific lines of dialogue where I remember reading reviews where someone was like, "That's such a Fraction line of dialogue," and I'm like, "I wrote that." [Laughs.] So it's kind of funny. Yeah, co-writing is a really mixed bag. Sometimes it's a lot of fun. And sometimes working with another writer, like someone like Matt, especially . . . I had a couple of ideas of what I wanted the *Iron Fist* comics to be when we first started, but I think it became a much more exciting, kinetic kind of thing, because Matt's energy brought that to it. And Matt was still really learning—I think at that point he had written two or three issues of *Punisher*—but he was still really learning the constraints of the twenty-two-pages-a-month Marvel comic, and how much you could or couldn't do. So he was trying to do so much within it, and a lot of what I was doing was cutting this or cutting that, but because of that, it gave us comics that I think had a different kind of energy than a lot of stuff that was on the stands. And he and I both really loved the idea of this previous Iron Fist, who then allowed us to bring in new pulp-universe kinds of characters.

So our sensibilities are really lined up on a lot of that stuff. It's like being in a writing room, sometimes. When you're co-writing with someone, it can feel like a hassle, and sometimes it totally just makes the story better. Same as having a good editor. Sometimes you're stuck on something and you call your editor up and you tell him what you're stuck on, and you kick some ideas around. Even if they don't give you the idea, the kicking-the-ideas-around-with-them part sort of gives you the idea somehow. It's like

House and Wilson. Wilson always helps House whether he means to or not. [Laughs.]

AVC: The most recent *Criminal* goes in a newly meta direction. What made you decide to bring in those *Archie* parallels?

EB: Well, it's more than just *Archie*. I'm going for a little bit larger than that. But there is an analogue kind of thing to it. I think part of it is that with *Incognito*, I had done a lot of little nods and Easter eggs to various things from comics and comics history, and pulp history, and I really liked layering in extra meaning into scenes, giving scenes two or three different meanings, so when you read it, thinking one way, you're like, "Oh, wait. He's actually saying he knows he's in a comic that's being read" or "Is that a nod to Grant Morrison, actually? Or Alan Moore?" I like being able to create something where it has multiple ways that it can be interpreted. I grew up reading *Richie Rich* and *Little Lulu* and *Archie* and *Binky Brown* and *Swing with Scooter*. All those teen comics, really. And when I think back to my youth, I think about those comics a lot. Like the Rankin-Bass Christmas specials and the *Peanuts* specials. It's just part of nostalgia for me. Cartoons and all of that.

My father was on his deathbed most of last year, and I was sort of wallowing in that childhood nostalgia a lot. And then this story just kind of appeared to me. Like, what if I did a story about these characters from this made-up, analogue version of a kid's comic, who all grew up? But they grew up fucked-up, because they grew up exactly like Dr. [Fredric] Wertham's worst fears of what kids reading comics would be. It took on a lot of different levels. And all of that stuff is really just the window-dressing for the story, in a lot of ways. To me, it's a really, really personal story about memory and the way we view our past. Idealize different periods of time that we lived through as being so much better than the period we're living in now. I agree that the '70s and '80s were way better than anything we're living through now, but while we were living through them, they didn't seem like the best time. [Laughs.] So I wanted to do something that approached nostalgia in a crime story. A crime story about nostalgia, instead of a crime story about sex or greed or anything. It's about sex and greed and murder, but the driving force behind it is also this feeling that you've screwed up and you wish you could get your past back to do over again.

And I really wanted to do a comic that didn't feel like a pitch for a movie. I've done comics that have been optioned for Hollywood, and I've done screenwriting, and I see a lot of comics coming out now that really just look to me like pitches for movies. And I wanted to do something that really only

Fig. 14: Riley Richards remembers his youth affectionately in the style of Archie Comics art and in opposition to his current life (understood with a long-shadowed noir filter) in *Criminal: Last of the Innocent* #3. (From *Criminal: Last of the Innocent* #3 by Ed Brubaker and Sean Phillips © Ed Brubaker and Sean Phillips; originally published by Icon in 2011; available in *Criminal: Last of the Innocent*)

works as a comic book, that uses the language of comics. That was where using Dr. Wertham's complaints from *Seduction of the Innocent* and having the
flashbacks be drawn in a sort of young-adult-comic style from the '60s or '70s
came in. I really wanted those elements to be a part of it, and to have that sort
of meta element on top of it. If you know about that stuff from comics, then
the characters can be viewed with extra meaning even though they're all just
parts of my own self and my own history.

I wanted to do something really ambitious. I really wanted it to be something that only really worked best as a comic. It's like *Watchmen*. Alan Moore
always said that people shouldn't make a *Watchmen* movie, because the things
that are most interesting about *Watchmen* are things that only make sense
because it's a comic book. The way it's structured, the way the stories are told,
the way the characters talk, the things they do. All of it really works best because it's kind of making commentary on comics at the same time. I wanted
to approach something that way, where it was really important that it was a
comic. I think I've accomplished that goal, at least.

AVC: On the subject of comic movies and the connection between Hollywood and the comics industry now, do you feel that the movies' influence can
sometimes slow the character evolution?

EB: Boy, that's a really weird question. [Laughs.] I don't think so. The main
thing, I think, is when comic-book movies are done right, they sort of tap into
the best things about the comics. Like, *Spider-Man 2* is the best of the Spider-
Man movies, and it really feels like that late-'60s, early-'70s era of *Spider-Man*.
Bits and pieces of that are in there. You can tell. I think the ones that are done
right become their own thing. *The Dark Knight* feels like various things that
have come out over the years in Batman comics. But ultimately, it feels like
its own thing. Anybody could watch it and not have to know anything about
the comics. I've never perceived any pressure . . . I wasn't at DC when *Batman
Begins* came out. I've never been working on a character that a movie was
coming out for until Captain America, and I never felt any pressure to make
it feel like the movie at all. I know from talking to people who worked on the
movie or saw the movie that the tone I established within the series was one
of the things they really liked and were trying to get across. I don't think
there's anything in the movie that actually reflects anything I've done in the
comic at all, but I think the tone of it is something they tried to get.

The reason we're trying to get Steve to become Captain America again and
having a new No. 1 issue when the movie comes out is because we'd be fools
not to. [Laughs.] But Steve was always going to become Captain America

again, and I was able to stop it for a while, because I still had more stories to tell with Bucky as Captain America. But I never had planned for Steve to not be Captain America again. It was always in the cards. It was always just sort of an accepted thing that this would happen by the time the movie came out, so there would be a Captain America on the stands that millions of people walking out of that movie theater might want to go, "I wonder what's happening in the *Captain America* comics?" And I wanted to make sure that the comic was something that would feel like, "Oh, okay. This is cool. This does not feel completely dissimilar."

If the movie had done something completely foreign to what we were doing in the comic, then we might have had a problem. But no, I don't necessarily see the comics industry trying to change what it does just to appeal to the movie market, as much as just trying to grab some of the audience of those movies and present them with good comics about these characters. I mean, the thing that it looks like was the biggest-selling Thor item around the *Thor* movie was the big Walt Simonson omnibus. Thank God, it's like a $75 book or something. But that was the book I saw everywhere. I saw Thor books at the bookstores, but that was the book I saw prominently displayed everywhere. It's like that just became *the* book. And that's stuff from twenty, thirty years ago. I don't see comic-book movies as a problem, necessarily. It's great if they're good movies, but hopefully it's something that will bring other people to the comics. I mean, after those Spider-Man movies came out, Walmart was carrying *Ultimate Spider-Man* paperbacks for a long time, and selling them to kids that had never been to a comic-book store in their life. I would see kids at the airport reading *Ultimate Spider-Man* for a few years after those Spider-Man movies came out. So the potential for that is great.

Adapting Your Own Work: An Interview with Ed Brubaker

SEAN HOOD / 2012

Originally published in *Genre Hacks*. 30 April 2012. Web. Reprinted by permission. Genrehacks.com.

Sometimes I do interviews on this blog in order to reach out to writers and filmmakers I admire. This is certainly the case with Ed Brubaker, author of the award-winning graphic novel series *Criminal*, as well as *Incognito* and the recent series *Fatale*. He's one of those comic book writers who, as the cliche goes, "transcends the genre" and gets reviewed in the *New York Times*. If you are a fan of hard-boiled crime fiction and loved the movie *Drive*, you should check out his work.

Hollywood has noticed him too, and much of his original work has been bought or optioned. This is pretty common for popular novels and comics, but what interests me is that Ed himself has been hired to do the screenplay adaptation for one of his most outstanding stories *Criminal: Coward*.

Readers of *Genre Hacks* know that I'm obsessed with finding ways for storytellers to get their original work up on the screen. Ed graciously agreed to answer some questions about the advantages and challenges of adapting one's own work from one medium to another.

SH: When you started writing your *Criminal* series, did you think of the possibility of any of the stories eventually becoming films?
EB: "Coward" actually started as a screenplay idea. But I could never find the time to work on it, and I kept having other ideas for the character and other ideas for crime stories, and really wanting to do a crime comic series. So I ended up taking the basic germ of it, and using that when we launched *Criminal* at Icon. When I wrote it, finally, like most writers, I hoped someone

might like it enough to make it into a movie. But I didn't write it as a "movie pitch on paper" like you often see in comics these past few years. I was building a world and exploring characters, and trying to make the best comic story, issue by issue, that I could.

SH: In my own career I been frustrated by the industry's focus on "pre-branded" material (sequels, remakes, and adaptations.) Many writers are now writing original books or graphic novels rather than original spec scripts. I'm thinking of David Guggenheim (*Safe House*), who made a deal to co-write his first novel, and Andrew Pyper, who just sold his unpublished book manuscript for *The Demonologist* to Universal. Would you recommend that writers with an original story should try to prove their concepts in another medium in order to build a following and prove that the story works?

EB: Boy, I couldn't say, really. I've been writing stories and comics for most of my life, so it's kind of all I know how to do. I always envied guys like Shane Black or Scott Frank, who got to write all these cool crime movies. I just always did comics, from when I was a kid, and always wrote fiction. When I was in my twenties, I wrote movie reviews and articles for a living, while writing and drawing my own comics on the side, because it was just something I had to do.

It's odd that we've ended up in a place where comics, which is a fairly low-paying field (compared to film or TV writing) have become part of the larger pop culture in Hollywood, and I feel fortunate now that pretty much every studio or production company has a few executives that are into comics. But that's a real recent thing. I was coming down here ten years ago, and that wasn't the case. Back then it would be someone's assistant, now it's the head of the company, sometimes.

But I've always thought, write the story in whatever medium you want to see it in. I did a pilot for Fox a year or so ago, and that was just an original idea I had for a TV show, not a comic idea or a novel idea. I think that's important, to respect the audience and the material. If you do a book or a comic that's just a movie pitch, it's unlikely you'll end up with say a Megan Abbott or Joe Hill novel, or a Neil Gaiman comic. You know what I mean?

So I would say, if you have an idea, make sure it makes sense as a comic, or a novel, or a web-series, whatever. Don't just take your spec script idea and shove it into another medium. Novels and comics and movies have totally different languages that make them all better at different things.

SH: Do you think we are reaching a time when it is common for the original writer of a book or graphic novel to also write the screenplay adaptation? (I'm thinking of Suzanne Collins and her involvement in the *Hunger Games* film.)

EB: I don't know. I think I would've sold some of my books a few years earlier if I didn't want to write the adaptations. *Incognito* sold fairly quickly, and there's been not even a hint of anyone wanting me involved in the scripting. Which on that one, I was fine with. But with "Coward," and most of the *Criminal* books, I either didn't want them adapted, or wanted to be involved, so I insisted. But I still get the sense, outside of independent producers, that screenwriting is this club that novelists and comic writers have to break into, through force of will. It's certainly not something most producers or studios will suggest. They'd always rather have their own people or a writer they know, doing that adaptation.

But you look at someone like Will Beall, who got his start as a cop writing a novel, then adapting that book—*LA Rex*—and then got hired on *Castle*, and now is a fairly hot screenwriter just a few years later. So it does happen.

SH: Your characters are seedy, complex, realistic, violent, and yet morally conflicted. They are not the kind of people we usually see in mainstream Hollywood movies. This will excite many movie fans, but does it make your producers and executives nervous?

EB: Not so far. The biggest thing I kept running into early on, when having meetings with studios about *Criminal*, was that they weren't "high concept" enough. I remember when we had a bunch of actors and directors interested in "Coward," originally, and we were taking it around, it was the same time the last *Die Hard* movie was a huge hit, and all the notes were—love the character and the world, but the heist isn't high concept enough, can it be about national intelligence or terrorism?

And then a few years later, you see movies like *The Town* or *Drive* get turned into fairly faithful adaptations of their source material, and do huge business. Affleck isn't stealing the Declaration of Independence or stopping a bombing plot in the *The Town*.

SH: Some of the best crime stories are showing up on cable TV, not in movies. In particular, I'm thinking of *The Wire* and *Breaking Bad*. There seems to a greater opportunity to write three dimensional characters, long story arcs, and creatively inspired scenes of violence and sexuality. What do you think of trying to take your work and, like George R. R. Martin with *Game of Thrones*, creating a cable series?

EB: I would love to, or to even create an original show for cable. With *Criminal*, I'm pretty far down the road on it as a film, but yeah, agreed. *The Wire*, *Deadwood*, *Breaking Bad*, and *Mad Men*, those are probably all among the best writing in the US in the past decade. If HBO or Showtime had come knocking for *Criminal* a year ago, I'd have happily said yes to a George R. R. Martin–style arrangement, where I got to be involved.

SH: You are working from a medium, sequential art, that is very analogous to cinema and TV. You already have dialogue, action, and structure worked out in your script for the comic/graphic novel. Your partner Sean Phillips, has already created an outstanding visualization. What is involved in writing the screenplay? Are you faithfully transcribing what you've already written/created or does a movie adaptation require you to make substantial changes to elements of story, characterization, or dialogue?

EB: That's the struggle I'm in, and why I'm not going to want to adapt all my own material, I think. With "Coward," the basic structure of the book is very much straight-forward three-act structure. And the director is a huge fan of the book and the way the story is told. He actually wants to be more faithful than I do. The things that change are, in the comic, there's lots of first person narrative explaining the world and the characters and the backstory, even their internal thoughts. You don't want that in a movie, not so much. You can do it; certainly *Fight Club* did it beautifully, and others have as well, but for a crime movie today, not so much. And some of the locations change, of course, and there are characters that are in the book that aren't in the screenplay, and some that aren't in the book that are in the screenplay.

And the main difference I've found from comics to screenplay with dialog is, in comics, you fake it. You try to write dialog that when read, seems in the reader's head to feel realistic. But if it's said out loud, it isn't. Because you're limited by space in the panel. You don't want huge balloons or tons of them all over the page (although it works for my friend Brian Bendis) so you fake it. But with film, the dialog can be more real. It's still not actually real, because that would be really boring, but you can expand it and find different rhythms and take more time with it. Something like *In Bruges*, what makes that film work, or *Kiss Kiss Bang Bang* (to name two of my favorites for dialog) would never work in comics. And that's why when in *Watchmen*, the film, when the actors said the dialog directly from the comic, it didn't sound right. Because those words were meant to be read, not spoken.

SH: Do you worry that the elements that made *Criminal: Coward* so effective and popular could get lost in the translation to film? What have been the biggest struggles in moving from one medium to another?

EB: The biggest struggle is second-guessing myself on every decision I made six years ago when I wrote it the first time. In some ways, I'd like to just pretend I never did the other version, and sometimes I'll be writing a scene, and then look at that part of the comic, and realize I did it better there. I think another screenwriter might not second-guess, and might just take the stuff directly from the book that works, because they aren't as close to the material.

My feeling is, I just want it to be a good movie. I already wrote the story one time the exact way I wanted to. Now I want the director and producer to help me realize it as a film, the best way it can be. The struggle there, of course, is they both love the book, and want to be faithful. It'd probably be easier for me if they didn't. Because I worry I'll turn in a script that's *too* faithful, and someone will think I haven't spent months agonizing over every scene. That I just cut and pasted the comic script.

And I also worry that part of what makes my comics what they are, my voice or whatever, comes in those narratives, which is what we're leaving out. I know it's not true, because *Gotham Central* was my voice, on my issues, at least, and we didn't use narrative on that series at all, but you know, I fear it anyway. I never want to write something that doesn't sound like me. At least, not anymore.

SH: It's extremely common for screenwriters to be rewritten by other screenwriters, especially as the project nears production and directors and stars are attached. Do you worry about your material getting changed in the development process?

EB: I do, but I'm not totally opposed to that, depending on the circumstances or the writer. My first screenplay was something I did for David Goyer about ten years ago, and after three drafts, another writer stepped in to do a pass, and it was weird. The story and dialog were all still there, but there was some new stuff, and he amped up the action and tension. I then did another pass over his pass, to make it more mine, and I learned a lot in the process.

But you know, once I'm done with my part, I know that's a possibility, at least, if not a likelihood. On "Coward," I am involved heavily and working closely with the director and producer, so I haven't worried about it as much. I figure if they need to replace me, it'll be because I failed, not because they need Scott Frank to do a dialog polish.

SH: While working on *Conan the Barbarian* I spent a lot of time rereading old pulp stories by Robert E. Howard and H. P. Lovecraft. I'm also a fan of crime fiction, particularly Chandler and Thompson. Tell me about how these pulp authors have inspired your work.

EB: I grew up on that stuff. My dad was a big reader and loved mysteries, and my uncle was a well-known screenwriter, John Paxton, who wrote *The Wild One*, and *Murder My Sweet*, and *On the Beach*, among others. So from a young age, I was always seeing old movies based on Chandler and Hammett books, and reading Conan comics.

As I developed as a writer, I drew from my own life, as well as all those pulp influences, to create whatever the hell it is I do. My real lightbulb moment was reading the Lew Archer books, by Ross Macdonald, because he was clearly writing about himself, while writing crime stories, too. And with Lovecraft, that's just the best kind of horror, isn't it? The kind Hitchcock would've done, where the anticipation is what drives you nuts, not the actual monsters themselves.

SH: Was the *Criminal* series inspired by any particular movies? Do you have any film noir favorites? What about current hard-boiled crime films like *Drive*?

EB: *Out of the Past* is probably my favorite movie. In recent years, yeah, *In Bruges*, *Kiss Kiss Bang Bang*, *Drive*, *Yellow Sea*, *Chaser*, *Memento*. A lot of others I'm forgetting.

But *Criminal* wasn't inspired by anything in specific, just a desire to have a place to tell all kinds of crime stories in comics. I was jealous of what Frank Miller had done with *Sin City*, but wanted to do something realistic, not over the top, and just wanted to write character-driven stories. With each *Criminal* story, there's a bit of trying to do my twist on a genre trope of noir, but I don't put too much thought into that side of it, honestly. I just let the characters tell their stories.

SH: One of the major reasons for *Criminal: Coward*'s success was the outstanding art of Sean Phillips. Is he involved in the film? Do you think that graphic artists could be a benefit to film production by supplying storyboards and production illustration?

EB: Sean isn't involved at this stage, but it may be something to discuss if and when we move to production. I'd hate to take him away from our comic work, on *Fatale*, but I do want him to have the excitement of seeing this stuff being brought to life, that he drew. If we actually get this movie made, I'm sure we'll both be on set as much as they let us.

Final Thoughts:

Besides being a Hollywood screenwriter and USC filmschool teacher, I'm also a fanboy, and I love Ed and Sean's work. It has all the visual storytelling, complex characterization, and tension-filled plotting that I aspire to as a filmmaker. The adaptation won't be easy, but it's one I'm eagerly looking forward to, and the producers made a smart move in hiring Ed to do the script.

Brubaker Drives "Fatale" into a Creator-Owned Career

KIEL PHEGLEY / 2012

Originally published in *Comic Book Resources*. 17 August 2012. Web. Reprinted by permission.

Though it's far from their first, second, or even fifth project together, Ed Brubaker and Sean Phillips's Image series *Fatale* continues to be a lynchpin title for the creators. In over a decade of creating comics together, the noirish horror mashup will likely end up being their longest single series collaboration. Last month, the title's first trade "Death Follows Me" hit stores, and just this week, issue #7 ramped up the snuff film facets of the current arc, which sees mysterious, cursed femme fatale Josephine come out of the shadows to drag a broken down actor into a world of cult intrigue.

Of course, for Brubaker *Fatale* represents a different shift beyond a new phase of his longtime collaboration with Phillips. The writer announced earlier this summer that aside from continued work on Marvel's *The Winter Soldier*, the success of *Fatale* has led him to do all creator-owned comics work for the foreseeable future. Combine that with a wave of incoming Hollywood prospects like the chance to draft a screenplay adaptation of his and Phillips's *Criminal* arc "Coward" for director David Slade, and the writer's career is entering a new phase after eight years headlining superhero books like *Captain America*.

CBR News spoke with Brubaker about *Fatale* #7 and his writing in general, and below, he digs into the differences his new '70s Hollywood horror story holds from the book's launch, describes some of the real-life occult crime that inspired him, announces a new run of one-shot stories that will expand *Fatale* beyond the scope originally anticipated, reacts to the massive amount of talk caused by his dedication to creator-owned comics, and teases where he'll go next in comics, film, TV, and beyond.

CBR News: With this week's issue #7, people are well into the second arc of *Fatale*. This story is a continuation of some elements from the last story, but in other ways, it's a whole new story with a largely new set of characters. Part of that piggybacks on the fact that, like a lot of Image books, you dropped a complete trade just before this story started. But I wondered if the clean break from the '50s story to the '70s story is just how you and Sean are used to structuring things since you worked on the more loosely connected *Criminal* books?

Ed Brubaker: Partly, I wanted to figure out a way to do an epic that had many stories within it. There are threads that carry over from each arc, but I wanted each arc to take place in a different time and a different location and even be a different kind of noir story to some degree. While I stuck to most of that plan, the characters started to take over. Josephine's life got bigger and bigger because there's so much stuff that happened between these two arcs that you haven't seen yet. I've got all that written in my notebooks, and I'm trying to figure out how to dole that out properly.

With each issue that I write of *Fatale*, I feel like the grand scope of the story gets bigger and bigger. We actually just decided last week that instead of doing only three arcs that tie together, there's also going to be four standalone issues in between the second and third arcs that all take place in different time periods. Those are about Josephine and other people, and they're all linked to this story, though they're important stories on their own. So now we're going to nineteen or twenty issues. [*Laughs*] It keeps getting bigger because my juggling so much between plot and character stuff gets harder and harder. The characters just take over, and I don't want to be forced by my own narrative structure to end it abruptly or push to a part of the story I'm not ready to be at yet.

This '70s storyline, some of the stuff that's in it is based on stuff I started researching twenty years ago, unbelievably. I had a weird obsession with Satanic cults and various multiple murderers in America. There's a lot of stuff in there that's been percolating in my head for years about weird cults and weird murders and Manson and Son of Sam—all sorts of stuff. Some of this is based on real stuff that actually happened. I'm just changing it to make it happen to new people.

CBR: I've always viewed groups labeled as "Satanic" to be more agnostic or pagan than people who actually believed in the occult, but lately I've read some accounts of the earliest followers of Aleister Crowley in California that portrayed them as really believing in the mythology of all this. What was your impression of the people in the real world whose lives synched up with what you were doing?

EB: Part of this is Hollywood. There was a lot of weirdness in the drug culture and sex culture of Hollywood in that era. A lot of that tied in with serial murders, and the Method Church in the book is my take on an actual religious order that was around from the '60s and into the '70s. Depending on who you listen to, Manson was a member of it, and the conspiracy that ended up resulting in the Son of Sam murders was part of their East Coast branch. There's a famous book called *The Ultimate Evil* by Terry Maury that's about the Son of Sam murders that gets into a lot of that stuff. But it also posits the theory that one of [Francis Ford] Coppola's producing partners on *The Cotton Club* was cut up into pieces and buried in the desert. [Film producer] Robert Evans had to testify at the trial, and it was apparently a coke deal gone wrong. But supposedly this guy was a collector of snuff films and was involved in Satanism.

But yeah, they call anything that's occult or weird "Satanism." I don't think it has anything to do with Satan or that anybody actually believed Satan exists. [*Laughs*] There's only like five people who believe that. Most of the people you meet who are supposedly Satanic, occultist people are like you say—agnostic weirdos who don't believe in heaven or hell or Jesus or God. It's more about questioning everything. But in this version of reality I'm writing, they actually believe in demons and worship various occult things they do sacrifices to. I like that creepy version of reality for storytelling. I don't believe in God, but I'll watch *The Exorcist* any day or *The Omen*. There is nothing creepier than the Anti-Christ. [*Laughs*] There's just something about that stuff, I guess because I was raised going to church, that has ingrained a fear in me.

So there's a certain amount of all that in this story. I'm trying to tie a lot of things together in my head as I make this story. I'm taking a lot of things I've always been fascinated with and putting them in a blender. I'm fascinated with *Rosemary's Baby* kind of stories and Lovecraft. I just wanted to figure out a way to merge those into one thing.

CBR: In this arc, our new male is B-movie actor Miles. He seems to function as almost an inverse to the men Jo met in the first arc because his life was falling apart when he met her. Her influence forces him to act in an almost more noble fashion rather than take his good life and shatter it as he fell for her. What about the era and the genre inspired that particular flip on the story?

EB: I really liked the "down on his luck" actor type, which you can only do perfectly in a '70s noir horror story. But I wanted to do this in a different way. Part of the power of Josephine is her effect on people, and I wanted to show how that effect could bring out good in them too. She's not just a corrupting factor where people abandon their wives and change their whole lives because they're under her spell. Miles is like a scumbag out trying to score drugs, but he ends up saving his friend from getting caught after she's essentially murdered some people. They stumble into Jo's back yard, and issue #7 was basically the story of Miles falling under Jo's spell. You follow him all day as he is doing uncharacteristic things and not understanding why he's doing them. I just wanted to take a different tack with it.

But then there's also Nick [in the present], and we're going to find things out about Nick in issue #8 because its opening is all about what happens to him after the beginning of the second arc when he realizes he's being followed by these creepy guys. And we'll also see Nick in the '70s as a little kid. We see bits and pieces of the guys from the first arc. The scope of this story and Jo's character lets you into so many worlds if you want to go there, and I love that.

CBR: It feels with each new story like we have two levels of players—people who are involved in the occult briefly and people who are possibly immortal like Jo seems to be. There are the men with the glasses and now "Hansel" who's the seemingly immortal master behind the whole conflict. Aren't you building the whole book around their stories too?

EB: Yeah, that was the big reveal at the end of #7. Hansel is the reborn Bishop from the first arc. He was reborn into Hank's baby! [*Laughs*] He was able to take over the body of this little kid, but he has no eyes. That gets explained more in issue #8—what happened when Booker, the cop from the first arc, cut the Bishop's eyes out. Him losing his eyes definitely comes around in a big way. I love leaping ahead twenty years to see what's happened to that guy as the leader of this weird religious sex cult.

CBR: And will all these roads lead to Nick's predicament for the series finale?

EB: Yeah. There will be a big modern story as Nick and Josephine meet again. He's been searching for her and getting close to her, but we won't see it until the final *Fatale* arc which will be all in modern times. Actually, I've been debating how that happens, so we'll see! [*Laughs*]

CBR: You recently did an interview with Tom Spurgeon at the *Comics Reporter* about the book where you revealed that you'll be going fully creator-owned outside *The Winter Soldier* at Marvel for the foreseeable future. And I've got to admit, I kind of assumed you were doing that anyway, so when that was big news, I felt like an idiot. [*Brubaker laughs*] But it was big news! Afterwards, guys like Grant Morrison and Rob Liefeld kind of got caught in the snowball you started down the hill by declaring the same thing for their careers. What's been your impression of the response you've gotten?

EB: I don't know. I was kind of afraid to talk about it even because I'm obviously still doing work with Marvel. They knew I was doing this. I had a long talk with [Marvel Publisher] Dan Buckley about where I was going in my career. More than anything, I've got these opportunities to write for film and TV that I've had things for years where a lot of things almost happened, but I couldn't really give my time to it because of my comics workload. So I wanted to pursue that stuff, and I was feeling kind of burnt out on writing superheroes anyway. *Fatale* being a huge hit was this great thing because it made me go, "Maybe I can just do a couple of the comics I own as half of my time, and then I can devote the rest of my work time to stuff I've been putting off for years and years." I explained all that to Dan Buckley.

And it was interesting because our interview happened right after the whole Chris Roberson thing, and everybody had been talking about these ideas. There was the scandal surrounding *Before Watchmen* and then Roberson's move, and then everybody was going "Brubaker's quitting Marvel!" I'm just ending my run on *Cap* after eight years and doing *Winter Soldier* for a while, but any new comics I do will be creator-owned. And who knows? Like Mark Millar has said in his interviews, sometimes it's fun to go back and do those other stories. Right now, my well is pretty dry on doing superhero stories. Honestly, I feel like it's been a struggle ever since my dad died. I don't know why that is. Just since then, I haven't had as big a jones for writing superheroes as I used to. When you're sitting there at someone's death bed, it starts to feel kind of ridiculous that you're writing stories about people who put on costumes and punch things to solve the world's problems. Though it's not as if doing horror stories is that much different. And I still like superhero comics. I just feel like I've written so many of them that sometimes you hit a wall where you go, "How many more stories can I do that end the same way?" [*Laughs*]

With stuff that's creator-owned, you can do anything you want with them. I never planned on doing superhero comics for as long as I did. I was just having a really good time and making really good living doing it. And it was really creatively fulfilling, but now I feel like the more creatively fulfilling thing I'm doing is *Fatale* and some other stuff I've got planned. I like having complete control.

I wasn't so much trying to make a huge statement as it ended up coming out as. But I'm fine with it becoming this huge thing. More people need to be reminded that you can do this. You can work for Marvel and DC to build up your name, and then you can get to the point where the audience will follow you from book to book. If you have an audience, you should take advantage of that by creating something you completely own and control. Gamble on yourself, basically. It won't always pay off, but when it does pay off, it pays for you and not somebody else.

CBR: Everyone knows you're doing more Hollywood stuff these days, some of which is adaptations of your work and some of which is original. How does that impact your comics work creatively? Will your comics be focused on doing something stranger as opposed to more realistic film projects?
EB: I've always tried to look at everything as "If I'm trying to pitch a TV show, what's the best TV show idea I've got?" I want to make sure that any time I do a comic, it takes advantage of the fact that it's a comic. That's important. I make fun of guys for referring to their stuff as "IP." But at the same time, one of my upcoming comic book properties is a thing where I was in a meeting with some producers, and they said, "We're looking for something like this," and I thought, "Oh shit. That's exactly what my next comic is going to be." And then I was thinking, "Can I presell my next comic?" [*Laughs*] Is that even something that's done? But then I figured Mark Millar does it all the time!

So I try to create stuff that's meant to be what it's meant to be. I don't think Vince Gilligan was thinking *Breaking Bad* could be a great TV show and a comic and a video game at the same time. My goal is to just try and write good things for whatever medium they're in. I got to write the movie adaptation for my own book [with the *Criminal* arc "Coward"], and that's really rare to sell your property to Hollywood, attach a director to it and then work with the director to adapt the book. But I got to do that, and it was a lot of fun. The resulting movie script is probably more faithful than I expected it to be because the director and producer both wanted it to be really faithful. But at the same time, there's a lot of new stuff in there because I had the freedom to do what I wanted with my world and my characters. Whenever there was a question about what did or didn't happen in the book, I just said, "I can just write it. These are my characters. I know them inside and out."

CBR: Okay, so the nerdiest question I can ask here is, does that mean the "Coward" movie will be "in canon" with all the *Criminal* books?

EB: [*Laughs*] No. No, it's its own thing for sure. That is kind of funny. There are some characters not in it and some who are. And there's new stuff that wasn't in the book, but it follows the gist of the book, basically. It was interesting to do, and I had a lot of fun doing it. But I have ideas for original screenplays too, and I've got blind deals for two TV pilots this year. Technically, that means I'll be writing two TV pilots, and one pitch is completely original while the other is based on this comic idea I've got. It's an odd situation, but I'm still trying to learn how to navigate these waters more than anything. It's a learning experience.

The biggest advantage here is that this is the best time in history to be a comic book writer transitioning into film and TV work. Everybody at the studios reads comics! It's really weird for me to walk into a meeting where there are already preexisting fans of my comics there. [*Laughs*] And also, they're fans of my less known comics like *Sleeper*. I'll go into a place, and someone tells me they like *Sleeper*, and I think, "Only 10,000 people bought that book. I guess all of them live in Hollywood!" That's a good thing.

The other good thing is that I'm not going into these meetings and worrying about whether or not somebody wants to buy my pitch. I don't really care because no matter what, I still get to write cool stories for a living. I'm not some waiter who's looking for their big break. I already get to write. That's all I do. It's a really big plus. Even if I were to sell a comic as a film or TV show, and the project is turned into a terrible movie or the TV show doesn't deliver on the concept, I still get to do the comic. That will always exist, and it's always an outlet for me. I'm not leaving comics for Hollywood by any means. I'm just taking the part of my life that used to be reserved for superhero comics and putting that time towards TV and film work instead. I still spend just as much time and even more time doing comics I own. I'm lucky as hell to have that opportunity.

I've been hemming and hawing about doing this for a few years, and I realized that if I don't do it now, I'm going to miss that time. I'd get to a point ten years from now where I'll really regret not trying to do that. But I'll always be a comics guy, and I've told Sean several times that no matter what, he and I are going to be doing comics together until we're old men.

CBR: Bringing things full circle then, whatever comics you have planned for the future I'm assuming Sean can't draw all of them. Are you looking to re-team with some of your past collaborators for more Image books, or are you looking for new artists to team with?

EB: I can't really say. Everything's supposed to be top secret right now, and I don't want to spoil any surprises or even get people speculating. But my goal is to have two comics a month every month. One will be by me and Sean, and one will be by me and someone else. Whether that means I'll have three or four other projects that are drawn by artists not as fast as Sean or two regular books, who knows? No matter what other stuff I have going on, I should always have time to write two comics a month. I've been working in comics my whole life, so I know how much time it actually takes, and two books is a comfortable workload. I've talked to Brian K. Vaughan about this, and it's his goal too to have a couple of comics coming out while he's working on Hollywood stuff. He works really hard and puts in long hours.

But if you can get two things out every month where it's exactly what you want and no one tells you to change it? I can't imagine what my life would be like if I hadn't met Sean way back when DC put us on *Gotham Noir*. Forming that partnership means that pretty much ten times a year for the past twelve years, I've had a comic come out that's exactly what I want it to be every time. No work-for-hire stuff that I've ever done is like that. [Steve] Epting and I did some issues of *Cap* together that were absolutely perfect—exactly what I wanted them to be. But there's always a fill-in arc here or there or advertising inserted in that you'd rather not have in your comic.

But while there's always something coming out from me and Sean, there's always a comic and a package I'm completely happy with. I like the paper and the design and the price point. I'm such a fetishist about print. [*Laughs*] But now I'm at the point where I'm old enough and where I've done enough writing that I only want to write the things I want to write. I've even turned down screenwriting gigs here that paid well, but I thought about it and said, "Do I really want to write this thing for two month? No. Something else will come up that's more in my wheelhouse."

I think a lot of that has to do with how long I worked on work-for-hire comics. Now I don't necessarily need the money. And thank you, Marvel and DC, for that! [*Laughs*] They did help me build up my name, and keeping the *Criminal* and *Incognito* books in print through Icon has let me be really choosey in my midlife crisis of wanting to change my career around.

Catching Up with *Fatale* Writer Ed Brubaker

MARK ROZEMAN / 2013

Originally published in *Paste*. 16 April 2013. Web. Courtesy *Paste* Magazine.

Paste: The past few *Fatale* issues have taken a break from the traditional structure seen in the first ten issues. Whereas the first two arcs alternated between the present day and an ongoing story set in the past, the last couple of issues have focused on different standalone stories set in different time periods. What was the decision-making behind that structure?

Brubaker: I felt like I had a bunch of ideas and mythologies that I wanted to weave into the story, but I couldn't figure out structurally how to do it within the tight framework of those arcs, with the opening and closing in modern times and having that chapter in the middle that's in modern times. I just love the structure and—I'm such a slave to my own structure sometimes—I really needed some other way to do it.

One of my favorite writers is Milan Kundera. I've always loved how he writes his novels in sections. Sometimes there will be a whole section that doesn't really seem to relate to the other parts of the book at all. And I thought, eh, fuck it, I'll just do a third arc that's just four short stories that reveal little bits and pieces of Jo's history and of the deeper history behind her curse—while also hopefully being fun, little horror stories. I wanted them to feel like old issues of *Creepy* or *Eerie* or something like that. I'm not 100 percent sure we pulled that off, but my inspiration was reading all those prints that had been coming out the last few years from Dark Horse. I'd been getting all the Bernie Wrightson and Richard Corben collections from *Creepy* and *Eerie*. I'm a huge fan of old EC [Comics] so I thought it would be fun to try to do something like that. And, man, I made it hard. [Laughs] It's ten times harder to write a single-issue story than it is to write a five- or ten-issue story.

Paste: How so?

Brubaker: Just fitting everything in. It's strange, I'm so used to writing longer pieces at this point that when I get to a single-issue thing, I always want it to feel like a short story. The biggest problem I always had with comics and that I've had from the beginning is fitting everything into the issue because (the issue) usually has a regimented page count. I always try to nail the twenty-four pages inside if I can, and a couple times we've gone like twenty-seven or twenty-eight, but usually I try to just hit that number. So that becomes hard when you're trying to build a whole world and a new character. So I just went with my gut on the issues. My favorite one so far was the medieval one. I think a lot of people love the Western one, but I wasn't sure if the Western one made any sense whatsoever. [Laughs]

The next [issue] is set in World War II and feels very Indiana Jones-y here and there, but also really creepy. And Sean's art in it actually reminds me of old EC *Two-Fisted Tales* in some places, so it's so much fun to see him do that stuff. After he started turning in the pages, I was like, "Oh man, we should do a World War II comic at some point." [Laughs] I think he would kill me if I made him do that much research every page.

Paste: Besides the film noir elements, *Fatale* incorporates a wide-range of different genres and styles. It's a Lovecraftian horror story, a Western, it has medieval swordplay . . . in many ways it feels like *Fatale* has become this outlet for you to create an amalgamation of everything you love. Would that be an accurate assessment?

Brubaker: Yes, the original goal was always to make it something like that, (something) that had a lot of elements in it that really spoke to my imagination. The initial idea for *Fatale* started out as a much bigger project about ten years ago when I was wrapping up *Sleeper*. I started working on a proposal for the thing that Sean and I were going to do next, that was going to be an epic thing that spans from modern times all the way back to the Trojan War. I had really grandiose plans for it and then, when I finally finished it, I kept looking at it and feeling like I was trying to be too much like Neil Gaiman. It didn't feel like me. While I thought it could probably be successful, I figured it would feel too much like work the whole time. It was one of those moments where I realized I was actually finding my own voice as a writer and that this wasn't exactly it.

The one part of it that kept sticking with me was the idea that one of the characters would be this archetypal femme fatale who lives forever; that kept kicking around in my head for years and years. I just kept thinking if there was a way to do the noir and supernatural, but also really examine the idea of the femme fatale and what she represents in crime fiction and what she represents in twentieth-century literature. She's mostly been a plot device and I really try to take that archetype and turn her into a person and tell the story from her point of view. I thought it would be a lot of fun, and then I could tell the sort of epic history stuff that I wanted to get into it.

One thing I really liked was that horror and noir were existing side-by-side in the old pulp magazines.

Black Mask and the magazine that H.P. Lovecraft and Robert E. Howard were being published in were sitting right next to each other. I was thinking, "Why didn't they ever do that back then?" I guess Lovecraft did a little bit of private-detectives-stumbling-over-things-that-drive-them-insane, but I just love that idea. I wanted to try to do something that reminded me of that old Mickey Rourke movie *Angel Heart*. I always loved that. I thought it was such a brilliant idea. It was one of the first movies I saw—way back when I was in high school—that blended horror and noir. I always had this idea to try to figure out a way to blend supernatural, demonic stuff with noir at the same time because it seemed to fit so well. They all exist in the shadows. That's kind of where it all grew out of.

Partly too, I think, when I started *Fatale*, it was going to be twelve issues divided in three four-issue arcs. I was about ten pages into issue two when I realized, "There's no way I'm finishing this storyline in four issues." And I sat down and was like, "Ok, they need to at least be five or six issues long" and I started expanding it. I realized, "Ah, this book's doing really well, why do I need to give myself an artificial ending?" I just decided, "Why do I need to stick to the old-fashioned way that comics have done things by announcing how many issues everything is going to be?" So that's why I decided to turn it into an ongoing series and just let the story tell itself as long as it needs to go. Once I decided to do that, I said, "Now I can do those single-issue stories." I can jump back into the past and explore different femme fatales and give it that epic feel that I wanted for it. It was really freeing to just know that I could do that too.

Paste: So do you have an ending planned out, or did that go the way of the former structure?

Brubaker: I know the end. It was more about getting there and realizing that I was going to get there too quickly, and I wouldn't have fully explored the idea and told the stories the way I wanted to tell them.

The next story arc was one where I was trying to figure out something to do for the '90s. All I kept thinking was "Well, should I just skip from the '70s

Fig. 15: After giving in to Josephine's seductive charms, an addled Hank is haunted by her presence in *Fatale* #1. (From *Fatale* #1 by Ed Brubaker and Sean Phillips © Basement Gang, Inc.; originally published by Image in 2012; available in *Fatale: Death Chases Me*)

to modern day as if nothing happened in America between then?" I think the next arc is actually going to be my favorite one so far because it's all '90s Seattle, and I lived there during that time period. I'm taking a lot of stuff that actually happened and blending it into this weird, noir horror thing that has like a failed rock band that now robs banks, a serial killer, and all sorts of stuff that I actually kind of lived through, watching TV or listening to the radio at the time.

Paste: It'd be like the Cameron Crowe movie *Singles*, but darker with more killing.

Brubaker: I lived in Seattle when *Singles* came out actually and we hated that movie. [Laughs] But we hated it in the way that any movie that takes place in your city is hated because you critique the continuity of things like, "How do you ride a bike downtown through Fremont and then Capitol Hill? What the hell? What way is she going?" It's funny because I used to live right around the corner from that building that [the characters] all live in in *Singles*.

But yeah, it's post that era. That was like early '90s, and this is more like a mid-'90s when the whole scene started to decay around the time of Kurt Cobain's death. But there's a lot of weirdness in the Northwest and I really felt like one of the things *Fatale* could do was sort of this James Ellroy–like examination of West Coast history. I like the idea of her going from San Francisco to L.A. up to Seattle. It just felt like a new angle of looking at this stuff.

Paste: You and Sean Phillips have been working together for some time now. How has that relationship evolved?

Brubaker: You know, it's weird. Sean and I have only spent time together three or four times at conventions or European festivals. Last time I saw him was around the time we launched *Criminal* and he and his wife came and stayed with us in Seattle for a week to do a convention. But yeah, it's weird, our relationship is almost entirely through email. But he's one of my best friends and we've been working together for twelve years. I started working with Sean around the same time that I got engaged to my wife.

We're at the point where, every now and then, I have to remind myself not to take him for granted because he's so fucking good and he's so reliable. The hardest part of doing comics is finding an artist that you love to work with who will actually turn in work. And Sean is a machine. The only reason the books are ever late is I struggle with the scripts or I struggle with a line of dialogue. I find as I get older, I write slower. But it's so easy to write for him, and yet I still remind myself every couple of months to try to push him. I think we try to push each other to keep experimenting and improving. It's a really good collaborative relationship. I would say we'll work together until we're old, old men and I hope that's the case.

It's a weird thing in comics because you don't see teams stick together for a long time usually. People always try to mix it up to get more excitement. But the way I feel, I want to buy novels from Joe Hill for the rest of my life. I like consistency, so that's kind of the goal and I'm just relieved that we found a big enough audience to support us doing it.

But yeah, it's interesting though, working with someone that long. Every now and then, I'm writing a page and I'm thinking, "Sean's going to hate this." And then I just do it anyway. I'd think, "Oh, there's way too many people here and tanks and Nazis." Then, I get it back and it's the best panel he's ever drawn and I just kick myself because there was a moment where I almost tried to rewrite it to make it easier on him. [Laughs]

Paste: Brian K. Vaughan and Marcos Martin recently released *The Private Eye* as a digital comic on a pay-what-you-want model? How do you feel about that model and is it one you'd consider for a future project?

Brubaker: I think a lot of us in the industry have been thinking about digital and different ways it could be used for our work. A lot of ideas being kicked around about its potential outside apps on the iPad. So to see Brian and Marcos just do it all themselves, just selling pdfs with no DRM, that's an exciting moment for the industry. Just like seeing Mark Waid launching Thrillbent was.

I actually talked to Brian about this a year or so ago and he told me what they were doing and that they were possibly only going to publish it digitally. I thought they meant they would only serialize it digitally. I still pray that they publish a big hardback of that one day because I'm a print guy. I'd never do something that wasn't intended to be printed, but I've thought about it for maybe serializing a graphic novel a chapter at a time so your artist can earn income while he or she is drawing it.

I wouldn't put it out of question. I love doing the printed books and my experience with digital so far has not been like Robert Kirkman's, where he makes a lot of money and sells a lot of copies of *The Walking Dead* digitally. Mostly I feel like the digital market for comics right now is still figuring out what it is. I feel like most digital comics are too expensive, especially since you're not actually getting anything. You're basically paying to read something and have it stored in a Cloud. It feels fake to me. When I first thought about what digital comics were going to be, I just assumed they'd be 99 cents because you're not actually buying anything. You're buying an experience. So I was surprised to see $3.99 digital comics and $2.99 digital comics. I feel like $1.99 is the most I ever want to spend on something like that—just personally. But it's interesting to watch it change. A couple years ago, we were all assuming that, within five years, the digital market would basically replace the monthly comics and then comic stores would all shift over to selling graphic novels and collections of the serialized stuff, but comic fans appear to like to buy print.

I love how the comics market has managed to get through a time when everyone was predicting its doom. With digital in past years, everyone's been predicting that it'll be the thing that kills comic stores, but it clearly hasn't. *Walking Dead* sells more now in comic stores than it ever did, and it's also the biggest selling thing digitally. I mean it also has a TV show.

Paste: That always helps.

Brubaker: Yeah, that really, really helps. I've been in the comic book stores when you see the wife buying every volume of *The Walking Dead* for her husband for Christmas and I'm just like, "Oh man, Kirkman, you lucky bastard . . ."

Paste: I was reading back in October that you were developing some projects with NBC and Fox. What's the progress on those?

Brubaker: One of them went through the development cycle back and forth to the point where, by the time I was actually approved to the script, it wasn't what they had actually purchased from me. So I knew that one wasn't going to go anywhere. That happens a lot, where you sell them the show and then, when you start turning in the outlines, they start having different ideas and taking your idea in different directions than where you thought it was going to go. So that was kind of a learning curve and that one didn't get approved.

I did one for Fox that went really, really well, but it was turned into Fox a couple days after the shooting at the Sandy Hook Elementary School and it was incredibly violent. We always knew it was going to be a long shot because it was about the Yakuza in Los Angeles, so half the cast would be Japanese. But, to their credit, everyone really dug it. The same thing happened to me a couple years ago when I did a pilot for Fox that everyone loved, and it came down to choosing between mine and a different pilot, and they went with the other one. They didn't pick up the other one either. So it's a weird market. When you sell a pilot, 90 percent of those shows don't end up on air. And they've all been paid for. So between all the networks, they probably buy about eighty or ninety pilot scripts. Of those, they probably make about twenty pilots. Of those pilots they make, they pick up about nine or ten. It's a really strange market. I have friends who make an incredible living selling pilots every year that never get produced. Or they get produced and don't get picked up. So, their whole career is writing things people don't see, but they get paid incredibly well for it.

I was actually relieved that the NBC one didn't end up going because it was so far from what I wanted it to be, but the Fox one was frustrating because we all loved it and we all thought it would be a great TV show. It was just way too dark and un-castable.

I'm working on a movie project right now actually, and then I'm going to be developing something for cable right after that. It has a really big director attached to it.

Paste: Can't tell me who?
Brubaker: No no no. I would be killed. [Laughs] Everything in this industry is so top secret.

Paste: What is the feature if you don't mind my asking?
Brubaker: I'm also not allowed to say what that is, but there should be an announcement about it in the next week or so. It's a crime/action/noir/horror thing. It's a job that I got hired for basically based on the script I wrote for "Coward."

Paste: *Captain America: The Winter Soldier* just launched production earlier this week. What hand do you have in a project like that, if any?
Brubaker: It's definitely out of my hands. [Laughs] But no, I got to go out to Marvel Studios a couple months ago and read one of the later drafts of the script. I went out to dinner with [directors Joe and Anthony Russo] and talked about the project and gave them feedback on what I liked or didn't like or what parts didn't work. I mean, the script I read was fucking fantastic. It was the best Marvel movie. It was really strange because [the script] feels like my comic while not really telling the same story as my comic. It's got moments here and there where I was like, "Hey, I wrote that." But mostly, it's not what people think it's going to be. But the tone of it was so close to what [artist] Steve [Epting] and I were doing on that comic in the first few years, where it feels like an espionage story almost more than a superhero story [and] there's tons of action in it. I can't wait to see what they do with it.

Really, it's just that the Russos are fans of my comics and wanted me to come see what they were doing. I got to see the production art and stuff, which looks amazing. And I knew the screenwriters; I met them at the last Captain America movie and we kept in touch. I live in L.A. now and work here so I've seen those guys a little bit. I'm going to get to go out to the set a couple of times during the filming. I requested if I could come out for one of [Robert] Redford's days because he's an honorary Brubaker and I wanted to meet him. But yeah, I think I'm going to get to go out sometime during the last week of April for a day and then I'll be there for part of the filming in May. I'll get to watch some stuff. But really it's just the Russos and Kevin [Feige] being cool and letting me come to see stuff that I created get filmed. It's pretty awesome. But I wouldn't say I'm involved or anything. I'm not a consultant or anything like [Brian Michael] Bendis was.

Paste: So if you had a cameo in the movie, you couldn't tell me?
Brubaker: I hope I get one. But I don't know if I will. I requested to be hit in the face with the shield if possible, but we'll see. [Laughs]

The Outhouse Interview: Ed Brubaker

ROYAL NONESUCH / 2013

Originally published in *The Outhouse*. 13 May 2013. Web. Reprinted by permission.

For years, Ed Brubaker was known as the popular comics writer whose work struggled to find a large audience. Though he wrote a Batman title for DC, his profile couldn't bring enough eyeballs to smaller, well-regarded titles as *Sleeper* and *Gotham Central*. Things started to change in 2004, when he signed an exclusive contract with Marvel and wrote an exceptionally well-received run on *Captain America*, one which lasted eight years. In that time, Brubaker found a way to resurrect Bucky Barnes in a thought-provoking and original way, bringing a new dimension to the Marvel Universe (it was also during this time when Brubaker made headline news for being the writer who "killed" Captain America). Brubaker's time at Marvel also saw him write a dramatic run on *Daredevil*, but most notably, he launched *Criminal* at the publisher's creator-owned imprint. Reteaming with his *Sleeper* collaborator Sean Phillips, *Criminal* was the place where Brubaker was able to luxuriate in his love for the noir genre, a love that shone through all of his books, both great and small (by the way, Ed Brubaker is the perfect noir name). In January 2012, Brubaker and Phillips launched *Fatale*, a pulpy horror comic at Image. Brubaker has also taken on a number of film and television projects over the years. He recently spoke to *The Outhouse* (over email) about *Fatale*, his writing, and how he woke up one morning with a bloody ear.

The Outhouse (OH): *Fatale* has run almost a year and a half now, and it's still going strong. Do you feel that it's diverged in any way from what you and Sean Phillips originally conceived?

Ed Brubaker (EB): I wouldn't say diverged, but I've discovered new avenues in it that I wanted to explore as I went along, so it's expanded a lot, but it's still heading to the same final destination.

OH: In general, how tightly are your long-form works planned out by you and your artists and editors? Would you say that you're an adaptable writer of serial fiction (in terms of being able to solve unexpected problems)? Is that a skill that you had to develop over time, or did you find that you had it figured out pretty early?

EB: I do a lot of notebook work on all my projects, some of it gets pretty detailed, but my outlines for each issue are always a bit rough, so I have room to change things or come up with other ideas if something feels off. I don't know if I'd say I'm adaptable, as much as I try really hard not to make a choice in chapter 3 that I'm going to really regret in chapter 10.

But I write almost entirely by instinct, and the only way I've ever been able to be productive is just to follow the characters to the scenes and moments that feel right to me. Any time I've tried to do something because someone else told me that's how it should be—like an editor or producer—unless it's one of those "Oh man, you're totally right" eye openers, I've never been able to make it work. Not to my satisfaction, at least.

OH: The themes you seem to come back to the most involve family or generational conflict, as well as conflict with one's past (also, the way those themes overlap). Having worked in that milieu for so long, has your relationship with those themes changed in any way? Are your reasons for exploring them now different in any way from the reasons you had earlier in your career?

EB: I don't really think about that kind of stuff too much. I always just start with a character or two and build everything out from there. But everything you write is a facet of your own history and life and regrets, etc. I just try to write whatever will keep me engaged and excited, honestly, and I like tortured main characters, generally. I think I write more about characters with fucked up pasts than fucked up family stuff, really, but like I said, I don't analyze it much. I don't want to wreck whatever it is that I do.

OH: Have you and Sean Phillips developed a kind of shorthand together in your collaboration?

EB: Yep.

OH: What does your average Ed Brubaker script look like? In general, do you give a lot of direction in your scripts? Do you write differently for an artist you've never worked with before than you do for someone you have?

EB: I don't tend to over-describe details, for the most part, and I try to make the scripts fun and easy to read for Sean or whoever else I'm working with. I don't dictate camera angles, but I will say if something should be a wider shot or a full tier panel, stuff like that. I try to make the visual something they can grasp and not ask for too much in any single panel.

And to your second question, yes, absolutely. Working with new artists is always a bit nerve-wracking and exciting at the same time. But I tend to write a lot more text on those early scripts, until I get the hang of how to write for them and what they do best. Sometimes what they do best and what I do best don't jibe at all, and that's happened a lot. That's why I stick with a few artists—like Sean, or Michael Lark, or Steve Epting. I've worked with them most out of anyone.

OH: Did your own artistic background give you a leg up on learning how to effectively write visually?
EB: I think so. Knowing how to draw comics helps you know what works, like how many people can be talking in one panel. I wrote and drew my own comics for a large part of my life, so I think visually, and I can often see the pages in my head as I'm writing.

OH: Fuck Marry Kill: Brian Michael Bendis, Grant Morrison, and Robert Kirkman.
EB: Uhhh . . .

OH: Moving along. Word is, you're doing some work in film or television. You're probably not going to announce here what any of those projects are, but in what ways do you think you're suited to those media?
EB: I'm old enough now not to take any of it too seriously, I guess, and thankfully, because I'll always be doing my comics with Sean, if one of my movies or TV doesn't get made, I still get to write for a living. But surviving thirteen years on the monthly comics grind certainly prepares you for anything.

OH: Do you separate story concepts according to what medium they'd be best for? Do you think to yourself "This should be a comic and this would make for a great serial TV or web series," etc. Do you generally come up with the concept first, or the medium first?
EB: I have ideas for TV shows and films and comics that are all separate from each other. I'm happy if someone sees something I do in comics and wants to make a movie or TV show out of it, but when I sit down to write a comic, I just try to make it the best comic it can be, and use all the language of the medium. I have had a few ideas that just sit in notebooks for years because I

can't decide what it is, but I think all three of those media are a lot different in many ways, and things that work in TV don't always work in film or comics, and vice versa.

OH: Considering the incentives you include in the *Fatale* single issues (a practice you and Sean instituted with *Criminal*), it seems obvious you're a proponent of serial comics being purchased (and read) in their single-issue form. However, you don't include the back matter in the digital version of *Fatale* either. That said, where are you on the state of digital comics today?

EB: We don't include the extras in the digital single issues because we charge more for the printed issues, and the digital comics apps won't let us price it the same. If they'd let us charge the same price, I'd include the extras in the digital singles, too. That's the only distinction, in my mind, and I want people who are paying more for the printed issues to get their money's worth.

Where am I on the state of digital comics? I'm not sure. Personally, as a reader I prefer print for books and comics, and I love big hardback art books like the IDW Artist Editions or Mignola's *Hellboy* hardbacks. I love the convenience of digital, certainly, but I have yet to lose myself in anything I'm reading on my iPad the same way I do with a printed book or comic. Other people love it, and that's fine.

I'm glad to see them available the same day as the print versions, because I think delaying them, sadly, just encourages people to steal them (and feel justified in doing so, like that guy who did the comic about how it's HBO's fault he had to torrent *Game of Thrones*). But I think the current model is a bit flawed, because I think the prices are too high and I hate all the DRM and how you're not actually buying anything.

OH: What did you think of the "pay-what-you-want" model Brian K. Vaughan and Marcos Martin (among others) have devised for their creator-owned work? Do you see yourself ever taking on something like that?

EB: I think it's great for them. I'm certainly supporting them doing it, as a fan and friend of both those guys. I'm glad to see some bigger names in the field trying it, and it's certainly something I've considered, if I were to do a digital-first project. I hate that they say they're never going to print it at all, because I want a big collection of it, personally. What I've thought about is closer to a subscription model, like getting X amount of people to commit to paying a dollar per chapter for a serialized graphic novel, and then publish a big hardback when it's all completed. Like I said, I love print, so I'll probably never do a digital-only project.

And really, I get so pleased when I go to people's houses that still have bookshelves full of books. Everyone super excited about digital books and comics seems so obsessed with "getting rid of their clutter" but you know what? I like seeing what books people own and what records they listen to. It tells you about a person. And I love borrowing a great book from a friend or loaning out a copy of a favorite novel. I'm not against anyone reading in any form, obviously, but I want to be able to make snap decisions about their taste in books, and now that's much harder to do. You have to hack people's iPad passwords and open their Kindle apps . . . it's no fun.

OH: Similarly what do you think of Mark Waid and John Rogers's Thrillbent, and the way it presents the comic book medium?
EB: I haven't checked out all of it, but again, I think it's great to see bigger names from our industry trying new things in that space, and I've been really enjoying *Insufferable*, although I'm a bit behind on it.

OH: Is it true you left Marvel because you're trying to destroy the comic book industry?
EB: That's what *they* say.

OH: Reportedly, you once had strep throat so bad that your eardrums burst. What? Seriously? That can happen? How??
EB: Just my left eardrum. I know. I had a bad strain of strep that kept coming back and finally my congestion got so bad my eardrum burst from the pressure. I woke up with blood crusted all around my ear.

OH: We at *The Outhouse* ruffled some feathers, yours included, when you were the subject of a parody article about the $3.99 price point in comics. In all seriousness though, from your side of the table, what are the real advantages of the $3.99 price point. Some fans try to make it correlate with "entertainment value," but how in your view does it serve the market to have single issue at that price?
EB: I am not a fan of the $3.99 price point, actually. When it was a few of their biggest books, and they all had extra pages, I was okay with it, but there are very few comics I think are worth $4 for twenty pages. The problem is, both companies did it, sales dropped across the board, and then when DC lowered their prices back to $2.99, their sales didn't go up. That's why the New 52 happened all of a sudden, to try to bring back all those readers they chased away from the habit. Now we're at a point where about half what they each publish is $4 and the rest are $3, so at least it steadied out a bit.

OH: Your uncle, the screenwriter John Paxton, was active in Hollywood during the Communist blacklisting, which ruined the lives of many in the motion picture industry. That said, wouldn't you agree that *The Outhouse*'s being blacklisted from DC Comics' press list is the worst thing that ever happened in the history of blacklists?

EB: I don't know, my uncle's best friends were some of the Hollywood Ten, who got sent to prison, which is probably almost as bad as being on a DC comics press call.

OH: The news about *The Outhouse* blacklisting came the same day as the (larger, much more important) announcement that *Comics Alliance* was shut down. What are your thoughts on the state of comics journalism, criticism, and discussion today? How plugged in are you to that space these days? In what ways is it strongest, and what can be improved? Is this something that creators, to your knowledge, think or talk a lot about?

EB: I grew up reading the *Comics Journal* and *Amazing Heroes* and *CBG*, and I think that kind of coverage about comics—reviews and interviews and analysis—is important. I found out about a lot of great comics because of it, as I'm sure tons of people do from the various comics sites and blogs these days. But I'm not very plugged into that world, really. I read a few blogs and comics sites now and then, but I find that as a writer, it's best to stay away from that stuff, if you can.

I get frustrated sometimes when I talk to friends who are writers or filmmakers who worry about some element that may offend a few commenters on Youtube or Twitter, because of how instant all response is these days. But you have to be true to your work. Some people won't like it, some people may hate it, some may misinterpret something a character says or does and think horrible things about you because of it, but if your goal as a creative person is to not offend anyone, you're doing it wrong.

Like, if Louis CK was putting *Louie* on Youtube instead of airing it on FX, he'd never be able to look at the comments after something like the "Blueberries" episode, which to me, was one of the funniest and most heartbreaking things I've ever seen on television. Just brilliant. But comment culture can be so kneejerk, it becomes like the thought police. So my thinking is, write your stories and take the feedback of friends or other writers you trust, but once you put it out there, you have to let people react however they react. That's how it should be.

OH: What does Brian Michael Bendis smell like?

EB: He has no scent, actually, like the guy from the book *Perfume*.

OH: Do you and Sean have any plans, even vague ones, to return to either *Criminal* or *Incognito*? If so, is there any kind of a timetable set for that?

EB: Definite plans to return to *Criminal*, still mulling over what comes next for *Incognito*, but no timetable. I'm still not sure how much longer we'll be doing *Fatale*.

OH: As a creator who has had success in work-for-hire comics, do you find that some of the pressures that come with publishing creator-owned comics are alleviated by the fact that you're kind of a "big name" in comics? Are there any pressures that are added due to your having that status?

EB: Publishing comics like *Criminal* and *Fatale* is just as much pressure as someone with a bigger known name as it is when I started out in comics. Actually more, because the artists are getting paid upfront, so they can devote their full time to it. You constantly worry you're not selling as many copies as you should be, or not doing enough press or that you should do more store signings. And getting the comic out ten to twelve times a year is a lot of work. People don't appreciate how difficult what Marvel and DC do every week really is, really.

Since we started *Fatale* at Image, our audience has grown a lot, but I don't think I'll ever get to a point where I'm not worrying about my projects being able to succeed. For me, success on those projects has generally meant making sure the artists make enough upfront that it's worth it, but now that it's my only comics work, there's added pressure. But I like it, I prefer the kind of projects I'm doing, and I like being in charge of paper stock and things like that.

OH: Some of us remember encountering a young Ed Brubaker in *Lowlife* a decade or so ago. Do you have a sense of how you might approach autobiographical work differently if you were to embark on a project like that today, rather than when you were younger?

EB: Not really. Everything I do has some autobiography in it anyway. I just grew more and more interested in noir and crime and mystery writing as a form.

OH: Do you think much about your life story, even in the context of your early work as a professional creator?

EB: Of course I do, I'm a writer. I do very little that isn't thinking about my life.

INDEX

CPSIA information can be obtained
at www.ICGtesting.com
Printed in the USA
BVOW08s0242081117
499834BV00001B/3/P